SLAVE STATE

Evidence of Aparthied in America

CURTIS RAY DAVIS II

MINDFIELD PUBLISHING
UNITED STATES OF AMERICA
Copyright 2019 by Curtis Ray Davis II

Mindfield Publishing is an imprint of Mindfield
Unlimited, LLC, New Orleans, Louisiana.

www.mindfieldpubishing.com

Library of Congress Cataloging-in-Publication Data is
Available upon request.

ISBN 978-1-7330616-0-5
Printed in the United States of America

ACKNOWLEDGMENTS

Bringing a project like this together requires the assistance of a team of people who do not always know that they are playing the major roles that they have played in the creation of what I hope to be a life changing publication. Naming everyone of these players is impossible. Just know that if your name is not here it has nothing to do with you, blame it on my head and not my heart. Allow me to begin by giving thanks to Allah, the Merciful Creator, through whose will has allowed me to pretend to have the power to create a book. I would also like to thank my mother Queen Ester Johnson, (RIP), who always insisted that I use my mind as my ultimate weapon. Much love and respect due, to Ofelia Garza, who made an awesome sacrifice to see me free, one in which I will spend the rest of my life attempting to repay.

Love and Light to my Family, Curtis Ray Davis Sr., (RIP), Joyce H. McKeever, my daughter Terquandelyn Kimble, Sophia Davis, Karen "Gigi" Floyd, Shajuania Smith, Tony Davis, Tim Davis, Troy Davis, Eddie Hobson, Ernest Wilborn, Quinton Watkins and Terry Davis for teaching me that blood does not define Family.

A very special thanks is given to Tiffany Lampkin Davis, who gave to me the greatest gift that any man can ever receive in the form of my new-born daughter, Queen Ester Davis. The system is partly designed to stifle reproduction and break family ties, you will never comprehend just how much you mean to me. A big thank you is also extended to my, stepdaughters: Kennedi and Kassidi Lampkin for showing unconditional love to an outsider the way that only children can. Special thanks to Lawanna Davis who has always been in my corner.

Peace and Love is extended to my Struggle Family: Fox and Robert Richardson, Anthony Boult, Rene Gummer, Corey Harris, Kim Floyd, Attorney Rachel Conner, Professor James E. Boren, Professor Andrea Armstrong, April Davis, Norris Henderson, Vote-Nola, Mercedes Montagnes, Promise of Justice Initiative, Innocence Project New Orleans, Louisiana Governor John Bel Edwards, Craig Lee, community activist emeritus, Attorney Jamilla Johnson, Attorney Kelly Orians, Participatory Defense NOLA, my entire Angola Alumni, and everyone involve in the worldwide criminal justice reform movement.

SLAVE STATE:
Evidence of Apartheid in America

TABLE OF CONTENTS

INTRODUCTION

H uman beings have been caging one another in dungeons for
at least the past six thousand years, nevertheless offenders
were often summarily executed or simply exiled to some
faraway wasteland. Historians have written volumes, on the subjects of,
punishment, social death and slavery. These scholars seem to agree by an
overwhelming majority that at the very foundation of our contemporary
system of criminal justice are two ignoble ideals: Retribution and Revenge.

Throughout time, mankind has demonstrated an almost demonic
inclination towards inflicting pain and suffering on his fellow man.
It seems only natural that to live in a civilized and ordered society
there must be penalties for those who offend by breaking just laws.
However, in a really, just society punishment for violations of the
societal contract would be meted out in a fair and balanced manner.
Unfortunately, this is rarely the case and to prove my point the reader
need only revisit what is arguably the single most striking incident of
wrongful and unjust punishment in recorded history: The crucifixion of
Jesus Christ.

Although it is glaringly obvious that Jesus was innocent of the heresy
for which he stood falsely accused, Pontius Pilate feared granting him
clemency due to the potentially negative political ramifications of such an
act. As a matter of fact, to absolve himself from the guilt of executing a man
he knew to be innocent, the Gentile ruler put the matter before the people.
When given the choice to spare the life of Barrabas, a known criminal or

Jesus Christ, the people in their amoral darkness chose to spare the life of a wicked man and sentenced God's elect to death.

As civilization moved forward the notion of incapacitating lawbreakers, or those who found themselves on the wrong side of the powerful and often corrupt lawmakers, grew from the traditional dungeon and execution to a much more brutal idea, the prison. In the 19th Century pseudo-humanitarian enlightenment had culminated into the advent of this new idea which came to be known as the penitentiary. Penitence sprang from the Catholic monastery model forwarding the motion of rehabilitation and repentance through solitude and isolation. Contrary to a belief that jails would reduce crime and promote right action, it has proven to be a severely brutal form of punishment, rife with corruption and inhumane practices that shock the conscience.

This book is an attempt to illustrate historical and contemporary failures in our various systems of criminal justice, but particularly the system of arguably the most diabolical design, the State of Louisiana. Slavestate, is a collection of essays and articles that I wrote while serving life in Angola Prison for a second-degree murder for which I was wrongfully convicted. I have separated the book into four sections; each section begins with a vignette describing an episode of my journey through the system. Each vignette is followed by essays that were written and published during my incarceration. My transition to liberty is contained in the epilogue, where I share the details of my return to society after spending 25 years and 9 months inside the bowels of a twisted system.

My intention is to answer two questions:
1. How did the State of Louisiana come to lead the entire world in per capita incarceration of her citizens?
2. Why are over eighty percent of her prisoner of African American descent?

Over the decades of my wrongful incarceration I discovered what I believe is evidence of a systematic practice of race based judicial discrimination, comparable to South African apartheid, being implemented right here in the United States. Welcome to Louisiana, come on vacation, leave on probation. If you're lucky.

Since love is the most delicate and total act of a soul, it will reflect the state and nature of the soul. The characteristic of the person in love must be attributed to love itself. If the individual is NOT sensitive, how can his love be sentient? If he is not profound, how can his love be deep? As one is, one is, so is his love. For this reason, we can find in love the most decisive symptom of what a person is.

"On Love"
— José Ortega y Gasset (1888-1956)

SECTION ONE

What You Won't Do For Love

I was arrested in Compton, California on September 18, 1990. The day started out normally, I woke up gave praise to my Creator and took care of the morning clean up. I was planning a trip to Houston, Texas, where I was working a deal with a club owner to promote a Hip-Hop, wet T-shirt contest. At the time I was employed as a data entry clerk supervisor for a company called, Cartel Insurance, while moonlighting as a Hip-Hop party promoter. However, before taking off for Houston I wanted to spend a bit of time with my little brother Eddie and take him shopping.

My parents were not married to each other when I was conceived. Queen Ester Johnson, my biological mother had an affair with, Curtis Ray Davis Sr., and produced me, Curtis Ray Davis II. It's a long story that is better suited for a biography instead of a collection of essays. One might say that my father was one of the early pioneers of the blended family model. I was raised in two different households, during the school year I lived with my mother, younger brother and older sister in Los Angeles, while in the summer I was shipped down South to live with my father, step-mother, and six half siblings. Two different households with two totally different sets of values and codes of conduct. Nevertheless, both groups believed in or at least professed a gospel of love, loyalty and familial trust. One of my father's favorite Biblical Scriptures was John 15:13, which proclaims:

"Greater love has no one than this, that one lay down his life for his friends."

It was from this binary programming, received in my upbringing that caused me to make the seemingly strange choices that were made throughout the episodes of my arrest, early interrogation and subsequent jury trial.

I was in California when I first learned that I was wanted on a Louisiana 2nd Degree Murder warrant. However, I wasn't really surprised because although I did not commit the crime, I knew all about it, as well as the actual perpetrator. On July 28, 1990, me and a small group of friends attended a dice game being held at a private residence in the Grimmet Drive Apartment complex in Shreveport, Louisiana. While in the small apartment, which had about 30 people inside, one of my brothers got into an argument about some keys he had lost. He believed that a gentleman by the name of Roderick Washington, who was to become the victim in my case had somehow stolen them.

Because I was well known as a promoter, the owners of the apartment called me into the kitchen and asked if I could control the people who came to the event with me. Although, I would live to regret it, my response was to let them know in clear language that I had control over no one except for myself and grown people must work out their differences between themselves. That said, the organizers promptly announced that the game had come to an end and asked everyone to leave the apartment.

As we were being herded out of the door a young man brandished one of those, black Tech-nine machine gun pistols, often sold at gun shows, and let off a fusillade of shots in the air that sent the crowd scattering in every direction. My guys got separated and me and my cousin Lonnie made our way down to the parking lot in search of my brother. Once we arrive, I was shocked to see that he and Roderick Washington, who was shielding a child behind him, were faced off in what looked like a fight about to take place.

I called out to my brother to stop the foolishness, unfortunately when he turned at the recognition of my voice, Roderick reached out and grabbed the gun and a struggle ensued. The weapon began to discharge and the only thing we could do is watch while the tragedy played out. All of a sudden, my brother shouts, "run he's got the gun!" Somehow, Roderick had taken the gun from my folks and was aiming it in our direction. Without much thought I took off running behind my brother, got into the car and rode away. I would find out later that Roderick had suffered a single gunshot wound to the abdomen that ended his life.

"I think he was hit." My brother's attitude disturbed me. He seemed to be thinking that this was not a big deal. He just got into a potential homicide with 30 witnesses present and its nothing. I told him to drop me off at my girlfriend's house. As soon as I got through the door, I told her to pack up because I knew it was time to get out of Louisiana.

That same night, me and my lady caught a cab from Shreveport, Louisiana to Dallas, Texas, where we caught a plane to Los Angeles where she and I shared an apartment. Within a couple of weeks, I learned that I was all over the news in Shreveport. The media referred to me as a Los Angeles gang member, wanted for the execution style murder of a rival during a robbery gone bad.

I learned much later, after my conviction that the Shreveport Police Department categorized the case as such to qualify for federal gang grants to grow their law enforcement budget. The war on drugs brought economic stimulus to the depressed criminal justice systems across the country. Billions of dollars were flying out of the U.S. Treasury to any county or parish sheriff and police chief claiming to have a problem with out of town gang members radicalizing the locals.

The problem with this categorization is that, although I am, "Straight Outta Compton", I am not, nor have I ever been a gang member. Of course, I have affiliations with many young men who were gang members; however, I was strictly forbidden by both my households form joining them. Hence the reason my mother sent me to spend every summer of my childhood in Louisiana. My influences come from more than the undisciplined streets of Compton, or the rhetoric and ideology of gangsters.

Anyway, let's get back to the story. I picked up my little brother to head to the mall before starting out for Houston, we were sitting at a red light at the intersection of Rosecrans Blvd and Bullis Road., made iconic as the intersection on the cover of Kendrick Lamar's "Good kid, Mad city" CD. When seemingly out of nowhere came the flashing lights of about eight police cruisers heading in our direction. In effort to give the officers the room they needed to get to their obviously important destination, I moved the car over to the right curb.

Suddenly, the thunder of helicopter blades shifts my attention and I look up to see a police helicopter hovering not more than a hundred feet above the streetlight. A figure in black Kevlar was hanging from the door aiming an AR-15 assault rifle directly at my front windshield. A guy gets on a loudspeaker and a booming voice starts ordering commands. "Driver place both your hands on the steering wheel! Passenger stick your arms out of the window!"

My little brother looks at me and I nod my consent. He complies with the officer's orders then I see another officer creeping up my side of the car. The booming voice continues with the commands. "Driver reach down and open your door!"

Growing up in Los Angeles in black skin teaches a guy a thing or two about police. The law enforcement officers of my era were notoriously corrupt and willing to use any excuse to have target practice on a "Brother", so I shouted back, "get the guy creeping up to open it, cause I'm not moving my hands."

The brutality of the city's police agencies was common knowledge to urban people, all across the nation even before the age of cell phone video or the outcries behind incidents like Abner Louima, Amadou Diallo, Sean Bell, or Michael Brown. According to a 2015 study conducted by the Guardian newspaper, racial minorities made up about 37.4% of the general population in the US and 46.6% of armed and unarmed victims, but they made up 62.7 percent of unarmed people killed by police.

If one takes a historical view of the experiences of Black people in America, the picture depicts the long dusty road our folks have traveled to reach the social, economic and civil inclusion that were and are still so elusive for the slave, Jim Crow Era Negro and even the post-Obama African American.

As the officer continued to creep up the side of my vehicle, thoughts in my head turned to my mother, Queen Ester, would always say to me, "you must take care of your brother, he is your responsibility and I am counting on you to look after him." Those words rang in my head as the chaotic scene played out around me. Here I am sitting here surrounded by an entire squadron of paramilitary police officers, who had in less than 60 seconds turned a neighborhood intersection into something resembling an Iraqi war zone, daydreaming about mama. I was literally snatched out of my musing, when the creeper cop grabbed my arms and yanked me straight through the window. My fall was broken when my shoulder smashed against the asphalt, I heard the pop sound of the bone dislodging from my shoulder socket about a second before I felt the excruciating pain that followed.

Somebody shouted something about me lying face down and spreading my arms and legs. I thought to myself, "can't they see that I can't move my arm?" A crowd of pedestrians had by this time gathered at the edge of the sidewalk I found myself looking up at. They seemed to be protesting the brutal treatment that had already been meted out to me. "What you think you doing to that brother?! He's not resisting arrest you don't have to kill him!" Thank God for *Vox Populi*, the voice of the everyday people. If not for these courageous bystanders, I could very easily have been the first Rodney King. One of the lead detectives saw to it that I was handcuffed and place inside his unmarked sedan. After his subordinates tossed me in the back, he jumped in the driver's seat and turned to me with a look of a satisfied hunter after a big kill. He wasted no time laying down the rules of engagement.

"I've been after you for a month. Somehow you always seemed to stay a couple of days ahead of me, but I Knew that you couldn't stay away from the people you love. I told my team that you would eventually visit your family. So, we staked out this house, the couple you have in Long Beach and even your sister's house on Baring Cross in L.A."

I was tired, and my shoulder was killing me and here he is exulting in his brilliance, hoping to learn more I asked him what crime I was supposed to be guilty of committing. He smiled in a way that let me know that he loved this part of the job.

"We have warrants on you for Grand Larceny, where you are responsible for the theft of seven high profile shipping containers from Long Beach

Terminal Island and the Port of Los Angeles. I know for sure that you masterminded those operations and you are wanted on a murder warrant in Shreveport, Louisiana, so I guess we have a lot to talk about."

I grew up in an environment where one is taught to never, ever talk to the police. There is almost nothing that can make an arrest better by talking to law enforcement without an attorney present. However, I noticed that a group of officers were placing my little brother in the back of a Lynwood Sheriff's squad car, so I asked, "You do realize that my little brother is a minor and has absolutely no involvement with any of this? I would appreciate it if you would release him and leave my car in his custody. Otherwise you can read me my Miranda rights and start processing me into county jail." The smile on his face grew wider, as though he had anticipated me saying something like that.

When he spoke again, he talked the way a seasoned businessman or negotiator would, "I heard you were pretty smart. We have reason to believe that you have illegal drugs, weapons and currency in that car. I am also aware that you have hundreds of thousands of dollars, worth of stolen electronics and cigarettes at your sister's house, among other places. I can lock your pretty brother up in the Glass House (LA County Jail), and we will see how well he fares with the hardcore bangers. I can execute a warrant on your sister and have her up in Sybil Brand (Women's jail in LA), by tonight. Now I know you don't want to see those two precious nieces of yours grow up in the foster care system?"

In spite of the situation and the trouble I was facing I couldn't help, but be impressed at how ole' boy had really done his homework, but some instinct told me he didn't have everything as cut and dried as he presented it to me. My sister Gigi, and her children were very dear to me and the detective's threat against them made the hair on my neck rise. I took a deep breath to calm the rising anger his statements provoked in me. The African Zulu tribe believes that the most, valuable, value a man can have is what they call "ubuntu", which in the original language of the Zulus. It means, I am who I am because of who we all are. The connotation extends the bond to include the good times and the bad.

Although I was not born and raised in Africa, my loyalty and commitment to family is as much a part of who I am as the blood that runs through my veins. The throbbing in my shoulder was getting worse, nonetheless, I went on with my mental assessment of what I can only call my dire predicament.

This guy is arresting me for Grand Larceny and Murder, he has an idea where some of the goods are being warehoused and he wants to use my little brother, sister & nieces as hostages to compel my cooperation. He seems to also believe that I see myself as smart. How can I sue this to my advantage?

"Okay, detective let's see you make a good faith showing. Get on your radio and tell them to release my little brother and the car."

His eyes seemed to transform right before my eyes into the retinas of a poisonous reptile. I held his stare and watched him weigh the pros and cons on the scales of his devious mind. By nature, he is a hunter and to bag a catch like me as a big deal, which he thought might lead to bigger fish. After wrestling with his thoughts for what seemed like an eternity, he reached down to the digital communications unit under his dashboard and ordered his team leader to release my little brother.

So far so good, I thought to myself. I was silent as I watched him get into my car and drive away. When I finally spoke, I was basically buying enough time for Eddie to get far away to a safe place.

"I did not kill anyone."

My declaration of innocence did not come as any great surprise to Detective Clark, I would learn his name later, his response did surprise me. "I know, because they have the murder weapon with your other brother's prints on it from the scene of the crime."

Then why in the hell am I the one wanted for murder? And why was the warrant issued for my arrest instead of his? I asked these questions to myself as I sat there looking into the eyes of this human snake passing himself off as a police detective. As if he could read my mind, the answers shot out of his mouth, burning me as though they were molten lava.

"Curtis, I don't care that you didn't shoot that guy. You're crooked and you steal. You know how the saying goes; If you lie then you will steal and if you steal, you will kill. If you have not killed someone by now, you will eventually, so getting you off the street is in the best interest of society. You people are out here wreaking havoc on the communities you live in and think that you're are the only ones who can break the rules and get away with it."

What is this "you people" crap that he is talking about. Okay I might have lifted a couple of containers of VCRs, but that doesn't make me a murderer. Then I said as much, "So, what you're saying is that you are willing to frame me for something that I didn't do because you think I stole some stuff?"

His reply was delivered in a clear matter of fact manner.

"Naw, what I'm proposing is that we help one another, and I might be able to convince the authorities down there in Louisiana not to give your stupid ass a million years. Now, I need information that might help me solve some of the crime going down around here."

This guy was really attempting to recruit me as an informant. He continued with threats about how if I refused to assist him, I would most likely spend decades picking cotton in some penal colony down south. I listened for a while and continued to weigh my circumstances. They have the murder weapon with my brother's prints on it, so they know I didn't commit the crime. How much does he really know about the containers? Can they really send me to prison for a murder that I didn't commit simply for refusing to become Judas Iscariot? If he knows that I have merchandise hidden at my sister's house, why haven't they executed a search warrant?

Well, I thought to myself, since becoming an informant is most definitely out of the question, I decided to let the chips fall where they may. I delivered my presentation as plain as I possibly could.

"Sir, I respect the fact that you have a very demanding job and must apply the tactics you deem necessary to achieve your objectives; however, it runs counter to my beliefs to gain peoples trust only to betray them to parties with contrary interest. I believe that my right to believe as I do is protected by the First Amendment of the United States Constitution and I am at this moment formally requesting that you read me my rights."

Then came that look. The dumbfounded stare, mouth forming an oblong O, then his eyes glaze over and the snake again becomes openly manifest.

"Before I read you your rights, I want you to know that you just made the biggest fucking mistake of your pathetic little life."

Essay 1: Barack Obama: The hope for a better world?

Last week the Honorable Minister Louis Farrakhan weighed in on the Democratic presidential nomination by making a statement that referred to the candidacy of Illinois Sen. Barack Obama as "the hope for a better world." The statement was carried by CNN, who found it newsworthy in a controversial sense – Black Muslim leader supports Obama. The news company failed to address the question, let alone answer whether electing Barack Obama president of the United States of America will bring about a "better world" and, if so, how?

The 2008 Democratic race for the White House has energized a debate within the Black community about our debt to the Clinton administration, a glass ceiling for African American political possibilities and low of Black people by Black people. This election has also exposed the effects of Willie Lynch programming that still orders the binary code of our mental operating systems: We lack knowledge of self and others and, as a result, we view the world through a warped perception of reality. Peep how Sen. Obama gained the majority support of the Black community only after white folks showed their approval by voting for him in large numbers. In other words, there are still a great many Black people in America who are so mentally destroyed and filled with self-hate that they cannot even in their wildest imaginations see a Black man a POTUS (president of the U.S.)

Scholars the world over have studied and compiled reams of data linking religious and racial symbolism and iconography to individual self-perception and worldview.

Acclaimed author and psychologist Dr. Frances Cress Welsing, unveiled a 10-year study on the subject in the 1980s in her groundbreaking work, "The Isis Papers: Keys to the colors," where she decoded the iconography and political symbolism of white supremacy.

Actor/comedian Eddie Murphy spoofed the study in a scene in the movie "Boomerang" when he and co-star Martin Lawrence discussed the color scheme of billiard balls during a game of pool.

Lawrence's character explained to Murphy's how the design of the rules states you can only win the game when the dominant white cue ball sinks the black eight-ball.

University professor and psychologist Dr. Na'im Akbar tackled the issue of African American self-hate with his book, "Chains and Images of Psychological Slavery." The point is that there is a vast body of work from psychologists and doctors around the world that support the theory that we still suffer mentally from our historical and contemporary relations with our former slave masters' and their children.

Now, what does all this talk of iconography and symbolism have to do with the question at hand?

I am glad you asked.

It is a well-known fact that African Americans are highly spiritual people. Most of us hold God (Creator) in the highest regard imaginable – Supreme Ruler, Sovereign Lord, etc. Of course, this would be all good and fine if mad men had not made graven images of humans with biological connections to heaven. What happens to the mind of the Black child who is taught that lighter skin is better or straight hair is "good Hair" and my personal favorite: The picture of the white boy hanging on the wooden cross as a representation of the biological (physical) son of God?

When those of us who love equality encounter these teachings and visual images, we regret them and the messages they intend. However, when we accept and believe these falsehoods, we lower our own self-perception in relation to those who share the physical characteristics of that image of God's biological son. After all, we naturally expect to look something like our fathers, and if Jesus was/is white, then it should reasonably follow that God must de facto be white also.

This is the "Mis-education of the Negro", that Carter G. Woodson warned us about. Remember, it is all about lack of knowledge of self and others. Self-hate is about lack of knowledge, just as self-love has a lot to do with knowing our history and heritage and caring about ourselves – in the words of the Honorable Elijah Muhammad: "Where there is no knowledge of self, there can be no love of self."

That said, what do we know about Barack Obama?

✓ He is the son of a white American mother and a Black African father.

- ✓ He was raised in Hawaii and Indonesia, blending in and soaking up cultural diversity like mother's milk.
- ✓ He was elected the first Black president of the Harvard Law Review.
- ✓ He supports shifting resources from destroying Iraq to rebuilding communities here in America.
- ✓ He has pledged to deal more justly with ex-offenders, providing funding for transitional jobs and social services for successful re-integration into society.
- ✓ He has worked as a community organizer in "the hood" on Chicago's South Side and, most importantly, he married a Black woman. Now that we have knowledge of self, let us get knowledge of others:
- ✓ In 1994, the Clinton Crime Bill was passed, earmarking $40 billion to arm, train and supply paramilitary police units that waged war on Black youth in inner cities across America.
- ✓ It was in 1996 that our "first Black president" passed the anti-terrorism and Effective Death Penalty Act, which bars a state prisoner's access to federal habeas corpus review of convictions and makes it easier for states to commit state sanctioned murders (executions).
- ✓ By 1997 the Clinton's were able to pass the Truth in Sentencing Act, which insures that an inmate serves a least 85% of a sentence.
- ✓ Between 1992 and 2000 the Clinton's were able to double the U.S. incarceration numbers from 1 million incarcerated when they took office to 2.1 million locked away by the time they left.
- ✓ Hilary Clinton is single handedly responsible for demonizing young Black men when she labeled us "super predators.
- ✓ America has the highest incarceration rate on the planet, and the Black community was disproportionately affected by the Clinton incarceration binge.

There has been a lot of talk about universal healthcare from both Democratic candidates and it is an indisputable fact that the United States of America is a very sick nation. Sen. Clinton likes to refer to herself as the candidate with solutions, smarts and experience gained from the previous two-term

Clinton administration. However, the Black community must be reminded that we were greatly harmed by the policy initiatives created between 1992 and 2000.

African Americans and Black people around the world can answer the questions by searching our souls and the souls of our fathers. As the iconography changes, our perceptions of ourselves change. The hellish, demonic bridges are replaced by infinite possibilities, respect for cultural differences and African American displays of human excellence. The world can only become better by replacing the icons and symbols that have caused hundreds of years of human suffering with the universal homogeneous icon of Blackness.

America needs universal healthcare, but she also needs moral healing, a refined image and universal justice. America desperately needs a facelift; the images of white supremacy must be replaced with the image of a Black First Family. When the people of America and the world look at the physical manifestation of Barack Obama, they see the color of long suffering. Picture the African nose and full lips and see how strong the victims of the trans-Atlantic slave trade have proven themselves. When people across the world see his genetic makeup, they know it offers a unifying element that fosters universal inclusion.

The ascendancy of Barack Obama to the seat that symbolizes the throne of world political power shatters the mental domination of our former slave masters and signals the coming of the kingdom of peace on earth. We can never have change if we continue to do what we always did and expect a different result – that is insanity, a psychological disease. I agree with Minister Farrakhan on this one: Barack Obama is more than a presidential candidate. His accomplishments and demonstrations inspire the best from our people. A President Barack Obama would mean 180-degree symbolic change. The world is looking better already.

Essay 2: Open Address to the Louisiana Legislature

Right on the heels of your recent special legislative session that focused on state ethics reform, your 2008 regular legislative session is beginning. The term limit legislation brought an end to the reign of lifelong Louisiana lawmakers: the legislative body is now comprised of 50 percent freshman.

Change is good, and Louisiana has a historic opportunity to atone for its past sins. and express its commitment to progress by fixing the policies that have held the state in the cultural, political and economic quagmires of the past.

Of the many issues plaguing the state, criminal justice reform is one of the most pressing. Louisiana ranks number one with the highest incarceration rate in the world. It also holds the title of the state with the highest crime rate, proving that incarceration and harsh sentencing do not deter crime.

Theoretically, punishment of an offender should try to achieve at least one of the following objectives:

1. Incapacitation: removal of the offender from the community to reduce the threat of crime.
2. Retribution: repayment of damages.
3. Rehabilitation: re-socialization of the offender toward more socially acceptable behavior.
4. Deterrence: discouraging the community from criminal behavior through public punishment of offenders.

Louisiana's criminal justice system and penal statutes were born from attitudes and beliefs rooted deep in the soil of Jim Crow policy and its subsequent political compromises. The laws still read similarly to the 18th century Black Codes, except only the current codes have substituted names and titles.

The attitudes, mentality, and prejudices of the framers of these laws are still working to the disadvantage of Black people and lower income whites. Although most of the men who designed Louisiana's criminal justice system are dead and gone, they live on through their legislation. This is the root of institutional racism in America.

Uniquely, the Louisiana judicial system is the only state system in America that does not follow common law this state's justice system is modeled behind a system of jurisprudence administered during the Roman Empire, particularly as set forth in the compilation of Justian and his successor, as distinguished from the common law of England and the cannon.

> During an era not long ago, a black person could be lynched for a violation as small as whistling at a white woman. Some of the framers of Louisiana law believed it was justice to incarcerate men for years as sugarcane slaves for "crimes" as small as vagrancy. Only a little hate, mixed with a little power conferred through elected office and the ability to write a bill, and voila: systematic re-enslavement of any offender caught in the trap. Most of the legislators who objected to such heavy-handed sentences were effectively silenced by the votes of the majority, who still held on to attitudes of confederate privilege.

Last month the Washington, D.C., based Pew Center's Public Safety Project released its findings from a recent study that 1 out of every 99.1 adults in the U.S. is in jail or prison. Whether we make the comparisons per capita or in raw numbers, the U.S., with 2,319,258 citizens locked up, incarcerates more than any other nation. Here in Louisiana, we incarcerate more of our citizens per capita than the so-called fundamentalists in Afghanistan, Iraq, Iran, and Pakistan. More of our men, women and children are behind bars than those in Cuba, Russia, South Africa, or even China. The U.S. and state-wide incarceration figures are bad because the justice system is rooted in immoral principles designed to hurt, instead of healing.

Further, the racial disproportionality in sentencing practices has not been seen since apartheid era South Africa.

Even after the Clinton administration's "Truth in Sentencing Act" in 1997, monies have dried up. Louisiana still has tens of thousands of inmates required to serve a minimum length 85 percent of an average 60-year sentence, which is 51 calendar years.

Men and women are serving natural life sentences – which amount to death by incarceration – for infractions as mild as credit card fraud

(See Mustapha Muhammad vs. State of Louisiana.) We have more first-time offenders serving life without parole per capita than any other state. Mandatory sentencing laws have tied the hands of state and federal judges, so they cannot – by decree of law – exercise judicial discretion to distinguish between the low risk offender and the truly dangerous predator.

For example, let us suppose, a 25-year old, nurse with no prior criminal history is being abused by her husband or boyfriend. As the abuse continues, she becomes so psychologically overwhelmed with fear of other assaults and desperation to protect herself and to end the abuse, she gets a gun, shoots and kills him.

This crime is second degree murder, but if properly charged and convicted, a judge is not allowed to take mitigating factors into consideration when considering sentencing. First, she acted from fear and desperation caused by the boyfriend's abuse. Second, she is not inherently evil. However, a Louisiana judge receiving a guilty as charged verdict in this case must sentence her to a life sentence, essentially death by incarceration.

These types of sentencing laws might be expected in primitive, unsophisticated tribunals or dictatorships; however, this is the United States of America in 2008, not 1808. Victims' rights advocates would have us believe that justice can be administered through a lens of vengeful retaliation; I am here to declare that justice demands a system of merited rewards or punishment.

Justice embodies the spirit and quality of being righteous, impartial and fair. Justice calls for the creation of laws that conform to an objective truth, reason, and logic. Louisiana's mandatory sentencing laws are both subjective and prejudiced – and prejudice means to pre-judge.

We cannot afford to allow our laws to be molded from the attitudes of vengeance, or administer punishment for the purpose, of inflicting pain and suffering. Louisiana's laws must be rooted in foundations of honesty, justice, dignity, equality, and mercy.

Louisiana needs a "five for one" good time act to provide a positive incentive for rehabilitating violent offenders. We also need parole eligibility for people serving life sentences. A law that provides an opportunity to evaluate the rehabilitation of offenders is not being soft on crime; it is being fair and displaying common sense.

How can we – in the 21st century with all these miraculous technological advancements believe that a fifteen-year old, who makes a mistake and who commits a crime should be sentenced to a prison term of his or her natural life? Think about your young, adolescent, likely immature, fifteen-year old. Are you the same person, mentally and emotionally, as you were at the age of 15, 17, 20 – or even 28 for that matter?

Louisiana spends only $4,000 per child a year for education for approximately thirteen years, but spends approximately $30,000 a year per inmate to incarcerate him/her for the rest of his/her life.

Can anyone say, "voodoo economics?" This is a real shame.

Louisiana is falling apart at the seams trying to recover from the devastation of two major hurricanes, Katrina and Rita and is squandering state resources by housing men that have been locked away so long that they have forgotten what they did. The price tags for our misguided policies are bankrupting the state, even fiscally demonstrating that substituting vengeance for justice is wrong.

As stated earlier, there is a purpose for punishment: correcting behavior and ensuring public safety. It should not be satisfying personal prejudices and perpetuating institutional racism. Change is good. Louisiana must institute a modern criminal justice system, employing a possibility for mercy and forgiveness, while doing away with the laws and policies born of the old, punitive and racist attitudes that laid the foundations for the current system.

Essay 2: Message to the Black Church

The 2008 United States race for the White House is being viewed by some in the African American community as a Divine sign: the breaking of the seven seals and the ushering of the Kingdom of God on earth. The truth of this may garner some debate However, it goes without argument that the Presidential race has reopened some very important dialogues across America especially where race, poverty, and discrimination are concerned. The media's verbal lynching of Revered Jeremiah Wright and the Black church image are telling signs that a culture clash regarding race is inevitable. With the forces of racism/white supremacy at play, the national Black Church community must work to increase its activism; after all, we fight not against flesh and blood, but against powers, against the rulers of darkness of this world, against spiritual wickedness in high places".

Principality means government. When the power of those in earthly authority become corrupt and engage in the oppression of the people they are sworn to serve, they represent "spiritual wickedness in high places." God is and has always been the God of the oppressed. According to Reverend James Halcone, the dynamic intellectual theologian from Arkansas, "The Black theologian must reject any conception of God which stifles Black self-determination by picturing God as a God of all Peoples. Either God is identified with the oppressed to the point that their experience becomes God's experiences, or God is a God of racism... The Blackness of God means that God has made the oppressed condition God's own condition. This is the essence of the Biblical Revelation. By electing Israelite slaves as the people of God and by becoming the Oppressed One in Jesus Christ, the human race, is made to understand that God is known where human beings experience humiliation and suffering... Liberation is not an afterthought, but the very essence of divine activity.

–From A Black theology of Liberation (63-64)

If when Moses entered Egypt to speak the truth to Pharoah he concerned himself more with being "politically correct" than carrying out the mandate given to him by God, Pharoah could have undoubtedly overcome him. It is the duty of the man of God to do the work of God on Earth and that work must be done without compromise or apology. Far too many of those of us who profess to love and follow Christ have opted to integrate into the wickedness of the world that God hates and has promised to destroy. In all actuality Jesus Christ was a revolutionary who embodied a revolutionary message; he ultimately implored those who would follow him to stop living on the low levels that they are living on and become an heir to the kingdom of heaven. Those who are in power and have authority are afraid of His message as they believe it to be a threat to their power; they subsequently develop a plot to crucify him.

A recent CBS news headline announced that Barack Obama has a new clergy problem and pointed to Catholic Priest Michael Pflager's parody of Hillary Clinton, mocking what many perceive as her **racist entitlement mentality** supported by white working-class voters who hold on to the mind-set that any white person would be more acceptable that Barack Obama, a black man. Politically, this is known as the "Bradley Effect," a study of the Los Angeles Mayoral election of Ed Bradley, which showed that some white people were willing to vote against their own interests because of narcissistic xenophobia that forces them to vote based on racial considerations, instead of qualities like competence, integrity, and honesty. Mr. Pflager has a right to preach what he believes to be the truth and his comments have unfairly been linked to Senator Obama. The way of God is not concerned with political considerations. The concern of the righteous servant of God is only "thus sayeth the Lord," while letting the chips fall where they may.

> Black people in America have a unique experience with oppression, hatred, terror, injustice, inequality, and dehumanization, unparalleled by any people in recorded history.
>
> It is only our steadfast belief that God is with us that has allowed us to make it this far.
>
> The Black Church is the last bastion of resistance to the devil's power to rule this world. It is our faith in God that brought us through chattel slavery; it was our faith that God is with us that gave us the courage to stand up to the segregationist water hoses, police dogs, and batons in our battle to gain Civil Rights. Now is not the time to put God on the back burner and make nice with

those that would have us follow them into the lake of fire or pit of hell promised to the followers of the beast in Biblical-Prophesy. The Black Church must continue in the tradition of liberation theology laid down by the prophets of God and righteous Ministers like Richard Allen (co-founder of the A.M.E. Church), Dr. Martin Luther King Jr., and Reverend Jeremiah Wright. And remember always that God is bigger than politics.

Essay 3: Message to the Black Church (Part 2): Innocence Matters

"From the dark energy of jealousy, hatred and envy was Joseph cast into the pit, then those insidious lies- the justification of his punishment – a product of his accuser's lustfully diseased mind, a world so insane and corrupt that her words alone were enough to sentence him to a lifetime in prison – wrongfully convicted of a crime he did not commit."

—*Alim Kenyatta*
Anatomy of a Wrongful Conviction

The biblical transcript of Joseph's false imprisonment is the earliest recorded account of how and why wrongful convictions occur. The scene is set in the historical Middle Eastern land of Canaan where Joseph lived with his father Jacob and their tribe. Because Joseph was so highly favored by his father, he attracted the envy of a groups of his siblings who subsequently initiated a plot to get rid of him. As Divine Providence dictates God allowed Joseph to be sold into slavery. In the words of his brother Judah, "Instead of killing him, let's sell him to those Ishmaelite traders. After all, he is our brother – our own flesh and blood?" Thus, began Joseph's steep descent into the dark world that is slavery.

Joseph is taken into the markets of Egypt (Kemet) to be sold like chattel or piece of property. He was purchased by one of Pharoah's officers who held the title of Captain of the Royal Guard. He served as a personal assistant to the Captain's family, and according to all recognized accounts he always interacted honorably.

However, one day while the Captain was away his wife sought to seduce Joseph into committing adultery, which was a crime in those days. Most scriptural accounts of the incident agree that the Captain's wife was a highly desirable woman and possessed physical characteristics that might be considered beautiful. Nevertheless, Joseph stayed true to his father's teachings and did not succumb to the temptations of weak flesh, thus rising to a higher moral/spiritual plane. (The commission of the righteous includes right action)

As the saying goes, "to whom much is given, much is expected," the Captain's wife uttered her lies and accused Joseph falsely. The credibility of her husband's lofty office, coupled with

Joseph's low social position ensured Joseph's fall into the abyss of prison life. Joseph, Son of Jacob, slave of Potiphar, became a number and was sentenced to spend the balance of his days in Egypt's imperial prison.

Now we come to 2009 A.D. and I am writing to you from the inside of the bowels of what many believe to be the real Egypt of our time. The United States of America currently has more of its citizens incarcerated than every country in Europe combined. According to various think tank reports, there are somewhere between 2.3 and 2.5 million people incarcerated inside U.S. borders. Not included in this number are the countless others being held in places like Abu Ghraib, Iraq; Guantanamo Bay, Cuba and the so-called "Blackspots" or "top-secret" classified C.I.A. prison camps under U.S. control in countries all over the world.

We will more than likely be arguing for years about whether or not all this "lock 'em up" mania is justifiable, but what cannot be disputed is the fact that the government does not always get it right. Of course, everybody convicted by the system is not innocent, but it would be insane to believe that they were all guilty. Let's assume for the sake of argument that we were not in possession of the biblical account of Joseph's wrongful conviction, or the evidence in the more than 200 cases of people exonerated with the help of the Innocence Project's work with DNA technology. Common sense dictates, that because human beings are not God and they designed this criminal justice system, then the system has real flaws. Because we know that people cannot be correct 100% of the time, let's assume we're right 90% of the time: with 2.3 million people incarcerated, approximately 230,000 wrongfully convicted mothers, fathers, sisters, brothers, aunts, uncles, nieces and nephews are in the system.

Some might say that our system cannot possibly be wrong that often. Well, let's pretend that humans pursuing convictions can be consistently right even 99% of the time. Sadly, that one percent amounts to 23,000 people who are being unjustly punished for crimes they did not commit, amounting to a humanitarian crisis of unprecedented magnitude.

"But the Lord was with Joseph in the prison and showed him his faithful love. And the Lord made Joseph a favorite with the prison warden. Before long, the warden put Joseph in charge of all the other prisoners and over everything that happened in the prison. The warden had no more worries, because Joseph took care of everything. The Lord was with him and caused everything he did to succeed."

Genesis 39: 21-23

While Joseph was in prison something miraculous started happening, he began *helping* with his fellow inmates, much like a modern inmate/peer counselor, tutor, or pre-release mentor. God favored Joseph with the gift of spiritual insight. Other inmates started coming to Joseph with their problems, and he would lend them an ear, often offering them solutions using the awesome power of *his* spiritual gift. One day two inmates with highly placed political ties came to Joseph asking for assistance in making sense of their trials. Briefly, one of the men was to be condemned to death (Egypt practiced capital punishment), while the other received a form of clemency and returned to work inside Pharoah's palace. Before the pardoned man, who was also Pharaoh's personal cup bearer, left the prison, Joseph asked him to remind Pharaoh about his wrongful conviction. Unfortunately, the man forgot to mention him, and Joseph languished in prison:

"Pharaoh's chief cup-bearer, however, forgot all about Joseph, never giving him another thought."

Genesis 40: 23

Why did the cup bearer forget about Joseph? The cup bearer enjoyed a solid middle-class existence and even though he had witnessed the injustice of Joseph's circumstance, he was not in a rush to protest, as the status quo afforded him a comfortable life. When he was in prison with Joseph, he accepted the aid that was given to him, but he demonstrated his unrighteous selfishness when he disregarded the good man he had left behind after his clemency was granted.

As the world moved on, Egypt's economy began experiencing its first serious downturns. Pharoah had a dream that he couldn't make sense of, so he called on his astrologers, magicians, scientists, and various other advisors. No one in the collective intellectual community of Egypt possessed the requisite spiritual insight needed to read the zeitgeist of the time.

It was only then that the opportunistic cup bearer remembered his gifted, benevolent mentor down in the belly of the imperial penitentiary. Finally, the word went out and Joseph was brought from prison to stand before Pharaoh. Joseph interpreted the dream, was subsequently promoted to a social position second only to Pharaoh himself, and averted Egypt from famine & economic disaster.

Joseph's contemporaries didn't have the Internet, and certainly did not have social networking platforms like Facebook, Instagram, Twitter, Pintrest, and YouTube. Had they known, they probably would not have protested much anyway, after all, they were mostly pagans who believed that things were the way they were, and nothing could change them.

Pharaoh to be a God that could do no wrong. In contrast, we now live in a time where 80% of the people on the planet claim to believe in a monotheism that states that the world was created by an omnipotent, omnipresent, spiritual entity that cannot be totally comprehended, but whom we refer to as God, the creator of everything. Some conscious people are therefore commissioned on a higher spiritual plane to stand up for righteousness and fight against the practices of the wicked.

So, what is to be done about the thousands of human beings languishing in America's jails, prisons, penitentiaries, and detention centers? Included within those ranks are the wrongfully convicted; we are the "Joseph People." Who understands their circumstances better than those of us from the black community? We have a unique experience of suffering unmatched by any people in recorded history. Most of us have had first-hand encounters with institutional corruption and know about the real-life horror stories that reveal the true nature of our modern criminal justice system.

If we acknowledge the collective legacies of our black freedom fighters & social justice advocates, who strove to fight injustice wherever they found it, we must also accept the fact that the black church shares a responsibility to stand up for the "Joseph People"; those wrongfully convicted, forgotten souls, longing for the freedom that is their natural right. In the words of the renowned Reverend Dr. Martin Luther King, Jr:

> We must use time creatively, in the knowledge that the time is always ripe to do right. Now is the time to lift our national policy from the quicksand of…injustice…to the solid rock of human dignity.
>
> *—letter from Birmingham jail*

We need the church to step up to the plate for greater social involvement and sound the call to raise awareness and/or concern about the existence of wrongful convictions: not just the one or two sensational cases that make the headlines, but the thousands that take place in those quiet halls of injustice. Somebody must speak truth to power and call out our elected officials who turn blind eyes to their corrupt colleagues who conduct back room dealings that undermine confidence in the entire system. Some officials use the righteous titles of their office as cover to perpetrate the lowest of crimes. We can no longer assume that just because a person holds an honorable title, that that person is in fact, honorable.

Public outrage at situations like the Jena 6 case, Sean Bell's assassination, and the exposure of Louisiana's 5th Circuit Court of Appeal's practice of a Judicial Holocaust on poor defendants has helped to shatter the illusion that these injustices "just happen."

It is the duty of the people who believe in the power of good over evil to help create a world of freedom, justice, and equality "on earth as it is in heaven." Understanding the enormity of this task, is why the job falls to the church. When a problem appears unsolvable or impossible that simply means that we're looking in the wrong place for the solution. As the scripture states, "we fight not against flesh and blood, but against spiritual wickedness in high places." Supernatural problems call for supernatural solutions.

I have served 19 years in this prison for a crime for which I was misidentified. It has been established that my trial attorney, turned *Honorable Judge Michael Walker*, accepted bribes to frame me for a shooting committed by my half-brother. As Divine Order would have it, my attorney was recently convicted and imprisoned for selling "justice" as a judge. My investigation was conducted prior to the F.B.I.'s and filed months before his indictment, but after sending the evidence to the Court, I was told that his Honor made my allegations un-credible/unbelievable. Now that *his* credibility and honor have proven to be less than that attributed to a common criminal, the state still refuses to grant me a new trial citing unfair procedural objections. What kind of judicial system says that innocence doesn't matter? Since when do the safeguards of appellate review, designed to ensure the integrity of convictions, need to be taken away from defendants in the interest of judicial finality? Since when did the court system, with its fallible and often corrupt officials become God? Returning to Dr. King's letter from Birmingham jail, he offers us insight in recognizing unjust legal practices when he says, "A just law is a human law that is not rooted in eternal law and natural law. Any law that uplifts human personality is just. Any law that degrades human personality is unjust."

They never have been and never will be God, so just like Joseph I will continue to work for a better world. My job title here in prison is an academic tutor; with my mind I work to impart onto my fellow inmates the ability to read, write, and solve mathematical equations. As a man who has been wrongfully convicted through corrupt judicial practices, I use my example to teach the world that nothing happens without the active or permissive will of God. Inside of man, is a Divine right to freedom that cannot be snuffed out by policies designed to keep truth from coming to light. I am a living symbol that points to the continued practices of those who use the justice system to commit legal lynching, resulting in the social deaths of those trapped by it. We deserve fairness in the judicial process. Procedural bars only work to cover-up injustice and protect those who practice corruption. As God is my witness, this case will be heard because innocence matters.

Essay 4: Parole Eligibility: A Safeguard Against Injustice

In Louisiana, a death row inmate who is wrongfully convicted stands a far greater chance of being vindicated than an innocent person serving a life sentence. In the cases of all death row inmates, some of the best legal minds in the country – coupled with international opposition to the death penalty – will work to ensure a miscarriage of justice will not result in the execution of an innocent man or woman. Furthermore, reviewing Courts will give claims from death row inmates closer scrutiny, reasoning that the death sentence demands a higher degree, of confidence that the verdict is fair and correct. This special interest is given to the capital punishment cases, because the convict has only two chances of getting out of prison alive; a Governor's pardon, or judicial reversal of the conviction.

The heroic work of organizations such as the Innocence Project, headed by DNA expert Barry Sheck, and the Northwestern Illinois Wrongful Conviction Center have exposed a startling fact about the United States Criminal Justice System: prosecutors do not always get the right person and Washington D.C.-based think tanks estimate that as many as 3.9% of people convicted of crimes across the United States are actually-innocent. In most cases, these are victims of mistaken identity, false testimony and judicial misconduct, and they serve decades behind bars in what one Texas man described as, "a nightmare in hell."[1]

Unlike those who are sentenced to death, a defendant sentenced to natural life must arrange private funding to secure the legal assistance necessary to demonstrate a wrongful conviction. Legal fees for collateral representation in challenging a natural life sentence start, in the neighborhood, of $10,000 and move up to around $250,000 depending of the complexities of the case. Of course, most people sentenced to life are poor to start with, and for them this price tag for justice is too high.

What may surprise some reader is this, a life sentence is legally defined as a quasi-death sentence." Instead of creating more safeguards to ensure those who were wrongfully convicted do not fall through the cracks, legislators have created procedural bars that prohibit the state court judges from hearing the constitutional claims of cases more than two years old.

There is a tradition in American common law that requires a 12member jury to unanimously find guilt beyond a reasonable doubt before a citizen can be sentenced to death or natural life in prison. After all, taking a life is serious business and should never be done on a whim as long as one or two jurors still have a reasonable doubt concerning the defendant's guilt. Down here in the Sportsman's Paradise only 10 out of 12 jurors need vote guilty to sentence a person to death by incarceration.

Legislation that bars judicial review of their cases or substandard requirements in jury verdicts help only in covering up injustices and aide in continuing the practices that cause wrongful convictions in the first place. Parole consideration and Post-Conviction Relief applications are the traditional mechanisms to aid innocent inmates lost in the system. Louisiana does not have a perfect or flawless legal system and should not make laws that reduce quality standards of justice. Parole eligibility after 15 years or so can act as a screening process to evaluate whether a person really deserves to spend the balance of his/her life behind bars. It does not just let ruthless people go free, because those truly dangerous to society will not be granted parole. With so much evidence that people are wrongfully convicted in thousands of cases, parole eligibility acts as a safeguard against injustice.

SECTION TWO

Vignette #2 – Angola Will Kill You

"*Man overboard!*
Who cares? The ship sails on. The wind is up, the dark ship must keep to its destined course. It passes on.

The man disappears, then reappears, he sinks and rises again to the surface, he hollers, stretches out his hands. They do not hear him. The ship, staggering under the gale, is straining every rope, the sailors and passengers no longer see the drowning man, his miserable head is only a point in the vastness of the billows.

He hurls cries of despair into the depths. What a specter is that disappearing sail! He watches it, follows it frantically. It moves away, grows dim, diminishes. He was just there, one of the crew, he walked up and down the deck with the rest, he had his share of air and sunlight, he was a living man. Now, what has become of him? He slipped, he fell, it's all over.

Around him, darkness, storm, solitude, wild, unconscious tumult, the ceaseless churning of fierce waters. Within him, horror and exhaustion. Beneath him the devouring abyss. No resting place. He thinks of the shadowy adventures of his limp body in the limitless gloom. What can he do? He yields to despair; worn out, he seeks death, no longer resists, gives up, lets go, tumbles into the mournful depths of the abyss forever.

O implacable march of human society! Destroying men and souls in its way! Ocean, repository of all that the law lets fall! Ominous disappearance of help! O moral death! The sea is the inexorable night into which the penal code casts its victims. The sea is measureless misery.

The soul drifting in that sea may become a corpse. Who shall restore it to life?"

"*Deep Waters, Dark Shadows*
From: Les Miserables
By: Victor Hugo

ANGOLA WILL KILL YOU

It happened in the predawn hours one morning back in February 1993. The cold air almost took my breath away when the correctional officers roused me from my deep sleep. I remember that morning because it was the day, I was to be transported to the penitentiary declared my final resting place by my trial judge. During the previous two weeks I had been housed at the Elayne Hunt Correctional Facility on the outskirts of Baton Rouge, Louisiana. The Hunt Prison is a Department of Corrections diagnostic center, used to classify the various convicted felons sentenced to serve any significant amount of time at hard labor. I was there awaiting transfer to the "Big House," Louisiana State Prison.

"Get your ass up. It's time to take the ride!" The 6ft. 2-inch African American prison guard's attitude reminded me of the sadistic overseers that Alex Haley wrote about in *Roots*. This slave master's foreman was operating on a system of hatred born from racism and ignorance. What is this guy's problem?

I sat up on the bunk in the cell and looked around the small space: blank, gray walls, simple white floor, steel toilet, my entire world for the past two weeks, 6ft. in width, 9ft. in depth.

"Wait a minute. I need to brush my teeth."

Before allowing him time to think that I was asking for permission, I grabbed my cosmetics bag and fished out my morning toiletries. Big boy just stood in front of the cell looking at me like his mind was troubled by my attitude. As I was finishing up and washing my face, he decided to engage me in conversation.

"I hear you're supposed to be, some kind of badass."

The smirk on his face communicated his thought that the brass at D.O.C. headquarters were most likely making too much of the "danger" a person of my stature could pose. I understood where he was coming from; after all, how much trouble could a 5ft. 7-inch, 160lb. guy, held in full closed custody cause? After looking in the steel slab above the toilet that passed for a mirror, I turned to him and asked,

"Was that supposed to be a question or were you just thinking out loud?"

For some reason, he took my statement as a challenge and before I knew what was happening, he held up a can of pepper spray and aimed it directly at my face. But before he was able to squeeze the plunger to blind me, I reached through the bars and snatched the whole can from his hand.

The look of complete shock on his face was classic, something akin to *Wiley Coyote's* realization when the *road runner* gets the best of him. He instantly jumped back from the locked cell door and activated the beeper on his waist to call for backup.

I sat down on my bunk with the can of pepper spray in my lap, waiting for the "goon squad" to execute what is informally known as a corporeal punishment session, when X, Y, and Z happen, but what is called a "cell-extraction." I thought to myself, "Damn! If it isn't one thing it's another. Should I fight or attempt to explain the guard's unprofessional behavior that caused this mess in the first place?"

After about 60 second of ruminating, I decided that I would fight. I reached into my toiletry bag and took out a bottle of baby oil. The sound of walkie talkies started getting louder, so I knew that trouble was on the way. I squirted the baby oil all over the floor to even the odds a little, then I applied it to my body to make it harder for them to get a good grip on me.

This was not my first encounter with a prison tactical unit. I understood that they would give me no respite and pull no punches; this was where the rubber met the road.

They arrived six-deep, uniformed in a manner that made them look like those auditioning for a NEW *Teenage Mutant Ninja Turtles* movie: Kevlar vest, combat helmets, jackboots and paramilitary uniforms. Whenever, they marched down the tier in lock step, the sound reminded me of the *Stomp! Stomp! Stomp!* The Praetorian Guard made in *Gladiator* when they escorted the Roman Emperor. However, unlike those ancient enforcers, these guys were armed with electric shields designed to send a high voltage jolt through the body of anyone unlucky enough to, come in contact, with them. With this fact in mind, I decided to wet the cell up with water from the toilet to ensure that whoever touched me felt whatever I felt.

Before they reached my cell, I heard somebody shout, "Rack open cell ten!" The order sent my adrenaline into overdrive, and I had to consciously seek out the mental void I used for meditation to bring my racing heartbeat under control.

Suddenly a calm, authoritative voice ordered the team to stand down. A white man in civilian clothing stepped in front of my cell accompanied by an attractive red headed female. She was wearing a D.O.C. uniform with a gold leaf insignia identifying her security rank as Major.

Mr. Professional looked me up and down and then his eyes peruse the cell, taking in my defensive strategy. "Looks like you intending to do battle with my tact team. I ought to let 'em come in there and break your ass apart," stated in a bland, matter-of-fact manner with no amusement.

So much for thinking of this dude as a professional… Nevertheless, I decided that I could at least try reasoning with him.

"Excuse me sir, but I am simply preparing to defend myself against being attacked by your tact team, because of the unprofessional provocation by the officer you have working this tier. Your man attempted to assault me this morning for no other reason than to show me that he could. And if these men enter this cell with the intent to do me harm, then I have a right as a human being to at the very least attempt to defend myself."

For a moment after I finished speaking, the two of them just looked at me with the same dumbfounded expression that I have seen countless times on the faces of people shocked to have encountered an articulate Black man.

"Boy, where you learn to talk like that? You got a lot of fancy words, but the fact remains that you have violated the rules & regulations of this here institution. Now as a warden in this facility I must ensure that defiant bastards like you are made to stay in ya'lls place." The gleam in his eyes told me that he had probably been, "at the lodge" recently discussing with his cronies, how niggers no longer knew their proper places in society. Of course, this was a golden opportunity for him to show my "uppity" ass a thing or two about the meaning of authority. Having divined his intentions, I thought it time to try a little charm.

"Sir, believe me when I say that I understand that you have a difficult job, and I respect your position as a warden. However, your officer was wrong, and you are the only one who has spoken a reasonable word since I arrived. I'm from California and things are different where I was raised. Could you at least investigate the incident before you pass judgment?" He gives me another smirk of acknowledgement and changes tact, "You tryna tell me how to do my job?"

"No sir, I'm just looking for fair and humane treatment."

Then, the female officer spoke for the first time, reaching out her hand to ask," Would you hand me the pepper spray?"

I rose to my feet and walked to the bars. Then I gently placed the can into the palm of her hand. She nodded at me as if to say, "Good boy," then turned to the warden.

"Well sir he doesn't seem to pose an imminent threat to himself or others, so I suggest we call off the cell extraction, write him up for defiance and put him on the transport to L.S.P." The warden grunted his approval. After staring into my eyes for at least a full minute, he turned and walked away. As if by some hidden cue, the ninja turtles about face and *Stomp! Stomp! Stomp!* off the tier. There I was, left alone with a woman for the first time in over three years. Her thirty-something years had been kind to her; she wasn't what I would call pretty, but she was easy to look at.

We continued looking at one another in silence when I noticed her steel gray eyes soften to a gray mist. When she finally spoke, her words sent a chill down my spine.

"I don't know how a person like you ends up in a place like this, but I do know that if you continue to think of this as a physical fight, ANGOLA will kill you."

Essay 1: I wish I would've Known Better

I write to free the ideas that swim constantly through the oceans of my mind. In addition, if you hold some things inside, they have a way of disturbing your health. For the past several years, I've been toying with the idea of writing an essay to express a general apology to BLACK

WOMEN for every wrong ever committed against them by anybody, anywhere on the planet.

I often find myself debating with Brothers who espouse the ideologies of writers and artists the likes of ICEBERG SLIM, Donald Goins, and Charles Avery Harris, and their patently dishonorable lifestyles, i.e. "Pimp Culture" or come up by any means mentality." In all honesty I also was highly influenced by those writers; as a matter of fact, one of the first books I ever read was *WHORESON* by Donald Goins, when I was about 10 years old. My older sister Shajuana was a subscriber to *Jive* Magazine, a publication marketed to young Black females in the 1970s; they had some type of agreement with the publisher to send four sample novels centered on the black experience to the magazine customers, glamorizing the exploitation of sisters via prostitution. In my youthful exuberance, I devoured the books and as a natural by-product, I acted out of a "Player Consciousness' in my interactions with peers and members of the opposite sex. Before we go any further, allow me to qualify myself: I grew up in Compton, California the eldest son of Queen Ester Johnson. Those of you who were adults in the 1970s might remember her as the, original "Los Angeles Welfare Queen." She appeared in newspapers and tabloids across the country, in articles illustrating the empire she built on a scheme she devised to defraud the California Welfare System out of close to $1 million.

From the time I first started walking I've been exposed to serious game theory, the techniques used by players to persuade an individual to adopt one's own way of thinking. I've been sexually active since I first entered elementary school and for a long time viewed the mental manipulation of unsuspecting females as a validation of my own manhood. By the time I was 13 years old, I'd seen, "THE MACK" and "SUPERFLY", at least twenty times apiece and was well on my way to being irredeemably indoctrinated. It's almost as though the media and my environment were programming me to hate the sisters. However, the love I had for my own mother and sister acted as a balancing influence, preempting any real follow through in becoming a professional pimp. As a matter of fact, I never *liked* the idea of exploiting females, and by the time I entered high school, the pimp was a weak character in my mind. Around the time of my graduation I began to really pay attention to the teachings of the Honorable Elijah Muhammad. I was completely enthralled by the dynamic oratory displays of Malcolm X and eventually the Minister Louis Farrakahn, whose words moved me in ways that Donald Goins, "The Mack" and "Superfly" never could. They taught me that 'a Nation can rise no higher than its women;' if they are held down then every member of the Nation will be down, for she is the primary teacher of the children, and thus the people.

It has taken me half a lifetime, coupled with a life sentence in prison to unlearn the lessons of my upbringing and early indoctrination, and adopt a new view/perception. I've studied the dynamics of male/female relationships and how those dynamics affect the inner workings of our individual households, the nuclear family, and, our whole society. I've heard the horror stories of domestic abuse, in the forms of physical and verbal torture, experienced by so many sisters, ranging from beatings and incest to murder and forced prostitution. I've read about the sacrifices our women made during slavery, how they would put themselves between "Master" and socially impotent Black men, exposing themselves to repeated sexual violations to save our lives or lessen various other punishments. And in present day, I've watched the Black woman struggle to raise children fathered by men too overwhelmed or weak to stand firm and soldier alongside her for the family's survival and social development.

Sometimes I find myself at my wits end searching for words to express my gratitude for the

Black woman's steadfast dedication to our survival and rise as a people against all the odds. As I said in the beginning, I'd thought a lot about a general apology; however, my next though is always, "What for?" Although I recognize the injustices perpetrated against Black women by various individuals, media, and even Government, I don't believe I'm qualified to make the apology that they deserve. (Look at it as one more reason we must all support the movement for REPARATIONS.) When a person apologizes, to a high degree that person is accepting responsibility for the, affairs, or condition he/she is apologizing for. Not to say that I don't personally owe some Black woman an apology; I do, and I'm taking care of those issues independently. But the overall condition has root causes far exceeding my individual culpability.

I was born into a misogynistic society and the sum-total of crimes perpetrated against the sisters was not committed by me. I've never raped, pimped, killed, robbed or slandered the Black woman or any woman for that matter, and I despise those who do. I simply wish that I had known better so long ago when I accepted the negative depictions, views and images without fighting for her honor. When I was coming up, a person couldn't make a negative comment about any female member of my family without it turning into at the very least a fistfight.

Had I known a little bit better, I could have stood up for all Black women as a testament to her loyalty, spiritual resiliency, and selfless sacrifice for her captured nation. If I would have known better, I would have argued the superiority of our civilization when Africa was governed by Matriarchal systems and how peace reigned as a result. I could've informed them about the courageous exploits of Harriet Tubman, who planned and executed missions on par with those of the modern-day U.S. Navy Seals or F.B.I. hostage Rescue Teams, using covert tactics that freed hundreds of slaves from the clutches of the Southern planters. I wish I would have known about sisters like Sojourner Truth, Angela Davis, Nikki Giovanni, Maya Angelou, Rosa Parks, Winnie Mandela, Athena Susulu and Assata Shakur.

When we lack knowledge, and act contrary to what is righteous, positive and progressive, we act from IGNORANCE. The old saying goes, "when you know better you do better." Now I know that a significant majority of African American households are headed by strong African American females.

I currently work as a youth counselor in one of America's premier maximum-security prisons, Louisiana State Penitentiary, better known as Angola. I've come into contact with sisters who, to my amazement, are holding down multiple jobs, raising their children and supporting their parents. Along with my brother/comrade Robert Richardson we've interviewed several hundred Black women displaced by Hurricane Katrina who, motivated to maintain their connections to family, friends, and partners being housed here, returned here from states as far away as New

York. After bearing witness to these constant displays of love and dedication, I've realized, Black women are not as much in need of an apology, as they, are in need, of praise.

In the book, *SALVATION: BLACK PEOPLE AND LOVE*, the acclaimed visionary author and intellectual Bell Hooks writes:

"If black leaders, mostly male, continue to ignore the valuable contributions to the stability of Black family life made by caring single mothers, they will undermine and ultimately destroy the valuable and essential contributions single mothers make as they strive to create healthy homes for themselves and their children. Obviously, given the odds against them, many single mothers give adequate care but are unable to fully create an ideal home life. All praise is due to working single black mothers and their comrades receiving state aid who manage, in the face of adversity and circumstances they cannot change, to create loving home environments. They need to be given grants to write the guides for their dysfunctional counterparts and for everyone parenting under the circumstances that are not ideal. These women are seers with wisdom to share without communities and the nation about the nature of love. Unrecognized and unappreciated, they do the work of loving everyday"

My own theological studies have taught me that paradise lays at the feet of the Mother and the secret to the Kingdom of Heaven is inside of the woman. Recent genetic research has uncovered that the DNA of every person alive on Earth today can be traced back to a single African female who lived approximately 200,000 years ago. They call her the Mitochondrial Eve. So, the next time you hear that the Black Woman is the Mother of Civilization, know that it's not just some cute catchphrase; it's the indisputable TRUTH.

Black women are worthy of praise, because first and foremost, without her, there could be no us – black, brown, red, yellow, or white. They are Queens in our midst, whether we find them in public housing projects in New Orleans or mansions in Pacific Palisades. No one has accomplished what they have or continue to tackle what they do. They've broken the glass ceilings of corporate America and amassed fortunes the envy of Greek shipping tycoons. They graduate from college and Universities in record numbers; some of the most profound scholars, intellectuals, politicians, teachers, and scientists are my sisters, African American Warrior Queens. They are clever creatures who through sheer drive, creativity, and vision are bringing about a new social consciousness in the United States that will ultimately re-order the planet. They are Oprah Winfrey with her display of entrepreneurial zeal and mother wit, Kathy Hughes whose Radio one/T.V. one empire is one of the hottest buys on the New York Stock Exchange.

She is Cynthia McKinney, who demonstrated true courage when she alone voted against giving

President Bush virtually unlimited authority in prosecuting his, "war on terror." She is also Debra Lee, who as President of BET is redefining how Black woman are depicted in mass media; she is Terry McMillan, Exhaling and getting her groove back.

Her name is Keisha, extending love and support to her brother locked away in prison. She is LaSonya, striving to empathize with a husband's need to save his own; Alicia Birch who believes "we choose the wrong baby daddies;" Kamiyah who's on her way to Cal State; Khadijah never letting go of her dreams; Joyce caught between the conflicts of being a mother to another women's child; April Meshelle, trying to stay true even through impossible odds for success; Charise who reclaimed her man from the streets and a life of addiction; and Sibil Fox

Richardson, mother of 5 boys, supporting a family and building a movement to free her husband.

Her name is unique. It's New African, born of dreams of a better tomorrow. We call her Quanisha, Porche, Alexis, Lexus, Mercedes, Diamond, Hope, Tawanna, Lawanna, Tasha, Shannon, Sade, Aiesha and Jasmine. She's a young woman named Terquanderlyn, who's lived her entire life without knowing the true paternal love of a Black man because her father is trapped in the bowels of Louisiana's "criminal-Justice" system. The Black woman continues to weather the many storms that this world's life brings, and out of the material scraps we've left her with, she has created a PEOPLE poised to assume the position of rulership promised to us in Biblical text. This African American female is a mercy from God to all of us, I am forever grateful to her and very proud to be her father, son, brother, husband, and lover. It is my solemn oath & declaration to Respect, Love, Honor, Cherish, and Praise her to my last breath. I DO LOVE HER, and whomever has anything negative to suggest about her, know that you are a coward & a punk and I'm at you cause the bottom line is SHE'S MY SISTER. All of em'.

Essay 2: Today's Black Woman

The 2008 presidential race has the potential of bringing into focus the, long ignored issues of misogyny in American society as it relates to Black women. It also provides an opportunity to redefine traditional views of beauty. Historically, European concepts of everything from parenting, family matters, fashion and the social pecking order have been the standard by which the world judges right and wrong or good and bad.

I can recall watching my own sister play with her Barbie doll when we were children. She would lament to my mother that she believed that she was not pretty, simply because she did not possess the features and characteristics of the doll. I would sit at the kitchen table confused as I listened to my mother's attempts to build up her self-esteem by praising her beauty, while simultaneously burning her scalp with a hot comb to make her hair straight like a European's.

My mother's generation, the "Civil Rights" generation, seemed hell bent on having anything that the dominant European culture had, regardless of whether what they sought was good for them or not. As a result, the African American Gen X population largely seems to be suffering from self-hatred and lack of esteem, which have ultimately proven to be detrimental to the Black Community in particular, and the entire country in general. What I mean is this: when the female in any society is held down – ideologically, educationally or racially – the entire society suffers because the female is the primary teacher of the children and thus the nation.

When any member of our society is taught that their value is less than anyone else's based solely on physical characteristics, our society is guilty of undermining the potential of human development in the world. Black women have proven their value time and time again over the span of recorded history. Their sacrifices, spiritual resilience, and nurturing have benefited every race and ethnic group on the planet. Most of the founding fathers of the United States of America were taught and trained not by their biological mothers, but by female African slaves – traditionally referred to as "Big Mamas" or "Mammies."

Michelle Obama as the First Lady of the United States of America allows people of color to look to an image of beauty that resembles their own physical make-up, and the possibilities begin to become broader, dreams brighter and expectations higher.

When the child in the projects of New Orleans can look at the first lady and see herself, that iconography alone works as a powerful antidote towards curing what ails America.

When the child in Botswana is considered as beautiful as the child in Malibu, we will have made major strides in developing greater human connectivity. When we look at one another and see that we each are individually unique, individually beautiful and individually blessed, our world will change for the better because only through tolerance and inclusion can we ever have peace.

When the Michelle Obamas and the Cindy McCains of the world are considered equally beautiful, without needing to of copy or emulate the physical features of the other, we will have

CHANGE WE CAN BELIEVE IN.

THE UPHILL CLIMB

They drove by night through the desert along the border of California Nevada, the cold evening climate change made her position in the trunk painfully unbearable. She had been tortured but, she was still alive, the ropes used to tie her wrist and ankles burned deep wounds into her flesh, the result of her constant struggle to free herself.

Finally, the car came to a stop, its driver and occupants disembarked. She could hear their muffled voices. The voices belonged to callous men, who would become her judge, jury and executioners. They opened the trunk and she looked up at them unable to bring their faces into focus through her swollen eye lids. For two days she was beat, raped, and questioned; now they intended to dispose of her. Together they lifted her out and dropped her to the cold hard ground, and just as quickly one of their members brandished a handgun and aimed it at her head.

The killer looked into her eyes, and the emotion of hatred boiled his soul, his hand tightened on the butt of his weapon and his finger jacked the trigger. BANG!

I woke up with a start. The dream seemed too real to be just something in my mind; however, here I was sitting up in the comfort of my bed in my father's home in Shreveport, Louisiana. My mind wouldn't rest, it was 2:00 a.m., I had school the following day, but I couldn't think about going back to sleep.

You see this wasn't an ordinary dream and to say it was a nightmare would be an improper description. Honestly at the time I didn't know what it was, but after sitting in the same position for about 30 minutes I decided to go and wake up my father and tell him about it.

My dad Curtis Ray Davis Sr. was a contractor raising a family of 5 sons and 2 daughters with his wife, Joyce. I knew that he wouldn't be happy to have to be awakened by his youngest son bearing tales about nightmares or some boogie man.

Nevertheless, I saw what I saw and tonight he'd just have to be mad because the lady in my dream needed help and I was convinced that somehow the events in my mind were real. I knocked on their door and

I instantly heard my stepmother's voice, "Who is that?" I'm like, "this Ray can I speak with yall?" Silence. Eventually, my Pops comes to the door and before he could frown, I guess the look in my eyes convinced him that I'd come on serious or what I believed to be serious business.

He invited me into the room and asked me to explain my problem, I went on to tell him about the dream I'd experienced. I replayed each scene to him as though I'd been riding inside the trunk of the car with her. He tried to allay my concerns by explaining to me that we all have nightmares and the usual parental free styling that most of our people use when they don't know what else to say.

After he finished his spiel, I asked him to call on the telephone and let me speak to her. He picked up the phone and after several attempts declared that she was sleep and promised that we'd try again tomorrow. I returned to my room, convinced more than ever that something terrible had happened and cried myself to sleep.

The days that followed were like a nether-world experience, I couldn't pay attention to anything, school, girlfriends, band practice, nothing. My father had been unable to contact her or if he had he wasn't telling me.

A voice started speaking to me, it told me, "be strong", it warned me that in order to survive that I must be stronger than I believed possible. The voice spoke to me from inside my own head, but instinctively I knew it wasn't my own thought. The voice was preparing me for a long hard road.

After two weeks my father called me into his room and before he said it I knew what he was going to say, so I said it, she's dead isn't she!

That was the first and last time I ever saw my father cry. He wrapped me in his arms and hugged me hard, his sobs stirring the entire house. When he pulled away and looked into my face, there were no tears in my eyes, he said, 'it's alright to cry' and I politely told him that I was never going to cry again. I turned and walked out of the house and went to play basketball with my friends at the park.

My Mother Queen Ester Johnson was found shot to death in the Mohave Desert by a motorcycle gang that stumbled across her body while running around the sand. She had gone missing for three weeks and her murder has never been solved. Memorial services were held for her in Los

Angeles, California and Shreveport, Louisiana. I sat through both funerals front row and didn't shed a single tear.

The reader needs to understand here and now that I love my mother deeply both then as well as now. However, our society reinforces in its male children the concept that big boys don't cry and that being strong is manifested in the outward showing of a bravado that isn't necessarily the true 'inside' sentiment.

I was 14 years old when my mother was murdered; I was never given psychological counseling, church counseling or any healing therapy to help me cope with such a tremendous loss. I simply 'protected' myself by closing off my emotions, therefore when my mother died something inside of me died.

After the dream I was never able to view the world the same again, the voice remained my companion. It exhorted me to be strong, aggressive, fearless, and bold. I'm 36 years old right now, and the clarity of my vision and the subsequent reality of its validity; still acts as a major landmark in my spiritual development.

My life has always seemed abnormally harsh, my losses have been heavy and at times my faith has been weak. I'm currently serving a Natural Life Sentence for a crime that I didn't commit and the fact that I still have my sanity is a testament to the Glory of God. For the past sixteen years I've struggled to understand the purpose for all my heartache, pain, and suffering.

I've racked my brain to comprehend how a compassionate, merciful God could be so harsh. When I lost my Father 2 years later to his bout with Diabetes, I almost lost faith completely.

However, the voice remained my companion, at my father's funeral I broke down and sobbed hysterically, I cried for my Mother, I cried for my Father and I cried for myself.

I mourned my compounded loses and I asked God 'why?', and the voice said, 'it's all going according to plan'. What plan? How can everything be so bad and still be the design of a beneficent plan? Jesus Christ stated to his disciples

"I didn't come from heaven to do what I want! I came to do what my Father wants me to do. He sent me, and he wants to make certain that none of the ones he has given me will be lost. Instead, he wants me to raise them to life on the last day. My Father wants everyone who sees the son to have faith in him and to have eternal life. Then I will raise them to life on the last day."

Each, and every one of us is born into this world for a specific purpose, and just as Jesus Christ was sent, we each have an individual obligation to fulfill that purpose. I've learned through my trials that God is preparing a people for his glory and in preparing us we are to go through many trials. This world's life no matter how long it last is only a brief moment in time, in all actuality we can't die because our essence is eternal. Death is only the beginning of another journey and is not to be feared or dreaded, after all according to the old saying; "you can't get out of life alive."

From our very conception the life cycle is an uphill climb; we start out swimming against 700 million rival sperm cells in a race to be born into this world. If you are here alive today, know that you are already a winner and a very special person. We are born into this world with tons of faith it's only after we start losing a few bouts that doubt begins to erode that faith.

That's the uphill climb! Can you believe in God even though he cannot be seen with the physical eye? Can you believe that this world's life is meant for more than just sport and play? We must, each of us find our purpose in this world. We are to study, investigate and make an earnest attempt to understand God's Creation. We have an obligation to live our lives righteously and give aid and mercy to our fellow creatures.

If we be the Disciples of Christ we must exhibit Christ-like behavior, we are to minister to the poor, heal the sick, help the deaf to hear, educate the dumb, and make the blind see, and give God the glory.

'HARD TRIALS ARE NECESSARY TO ESTABLISH TRUTH.'

These trials aid in the purification of the human soul and are key to our salvation. So, when misfortune enters your life don't curse God, know that everything is in Divine order and trust that all is going according to plan. I Am Enduring, Dynamic and Divine.

Essay 4: Crime is a social disease

During the late 1960's, the legendary reggae artist Bob Marley penned a now classic ode to society's protected era of oppression and war. He titled the song "So much trouble in the world" and painted a picture of what happens when a legal system is used as a weapon instead of as an apparatus for justice. He performed with a fire and zeal that makes one feel a spiritual connection to those forgotten men, women, and children living outside the margins of society. Rhythm imparting a deep understanding of life's ups and downs; the vibration of the drum feeding insight to the politically blind. His words served as an indictment to the rulers of the people: those few responsible for widespread suffering. His lyrics offered a glimpse into the underbelly of the legal system. Oh! So much trouble in the World!

Thirty-nine years later, indeed much has changed: The Soviet Union has dissolved, apartheid in South Africa has ended and Nelson Mandela is free. All around the world wonderful new technologies have improved the quality of life for millions of people. Nevertheless, "the more things change the more they remain the same." And there is still so much trouble in the world.

Right here in the United States, which is probably the richest most technologically advanced society in the history of mankind, there are still massive concentrations of third world level poverty. In cities and towns stretching from the Appalachian Mountains to New Orleans, U.S. citizens are depressed and barely making ends meet.

More than a decade after the Soviet Union released its iron hold on the title of world's largest incarcerator, the United States is locking away more of her citizens than every country in Europe combined. According to the Pew Charitable Trust, the national prison population has nearly tripled in the twenty-year period between 1987 and 2007. There are currently 2.3 million people living behind bars in the "land of the free;" one in every 100 adults in the country. In the state of Louisiana, the number is one in 32 and that leads the entire planet.

The United States Department of Justice data shows that one in 106 white males are incarcerated across the nation. It is an extremely suspicious statistic when viewed in contrast to the one in nine black males locked away. However, no statistic can rival Louisiana's record down here in the "boot:" one in every four black males aged 18 to 34 live behind bars. So much trouble...

The Sentencing Project, a Washington D.C. think tank, looked at the numbers from different perspectives and found that the incarceration rates for whites in this country is 412 per 100,000. The rate for blacks is a staggering 2,290 per 100,000. Oh! So much trouble...

It is a reasonable proposition that responsible adults be held accountable for their actions, and punishments be administered to correct behavior, facilitating a just and peaceful society. However, we cannot disregard the fact that for decades racial prejudice and the criminal justice system worked hand in hand, and major injustices have occurred as a result. There are still powerful people who argue that young black males are genetically prone to criminal behavior. Bell Curve debaters are viewing America's incarceration binge as a "Final Solution" to the nation's "Negro problem." It can be likened to the old lynch mob mentality, but now on steroids. "When attitudes harden, they become beliefs and beliefs are subsequently codified into law."

Look at the trouble we are in. The momentum towards punishment over rehabilitation has kept us moving through a cradle to prison pipeline. I personally know men in their 40's and 50's who have not been free since they were 15 years old. The vast majority of those convicted and sentenced to serve time in this country are the poorest and most marginalized. Black people are not locked away at such astronomical rates because of some genetic short coming. This condition is the result of under-funded, public school systems, skyrocketing urban unemployment and deplorable living environments. Of course, the decimation of the Black family is attributable to over 400 years of chattel slavery and Jim Crow segregation. Therefore, it is safe to say our current inner-city crime problems are the negative side effects of social disorganization, judicial vengeance, and the boogie man myth. It is time to shatter the myths and change the condition.

When 70% of African American children are born to single mothers, they are victims of a social disease.

When we listen to mainstream radio and hear broadcast personalities encouraging our middle schoolers to "do your thug thang" or "back that thang up," we are hearing the perpetuation of an epidemic.

When you grow up in a single parent home and that parent is a drug addict, you are a victim of a social disease.

If you practice a culture that glorifies senseless violence through art and entertainment programming, you live in a culture guilty of incubating a pandemic social disease. Three decades of "get tough on crime" legislation has only exacerbated the problem, stripping communities of vital human resources. After being rehabilitated, men should be given an opportunity to atone by rebuilding these communities. Louisiana State Prison houses thousands of the most rehabilitated men in the United States, yet there is no viable release mechanism that will allow even a consideration of parole. Almost a thousand have obtained a college degree since their incarceration. Thousands of others have newly acquired vocational training qualifying them as welders, electricians, cooks, press operators and landscape architects. Angola has gained national attention for its correctional program called "Moral Rehabilitation," which is helping to transform thugs and hoodlums into caring, compassionate, human beings. The state-wide recidivism rate is 57% but the recidivism rate for those that leave Angola is less than 10%.

The advancements made by the prisoners of Louisiana State Prison are evidence that policies that concentrate on correcting behavior are better than punishment for punishment's sake. Our doctors, of law, and political science must re-evaluate the data because just locking up people will not solve our crime problems. The Criminal Justice System must be reformed and brought into alignment with the scientific evidence that shows that moral rehabilitation works. Louisiana lifers' and long termers must be granted an opportunity to present our new attitudes, credentials, and qualifications to the parole board that some of us may be allowed to re-enter society as rebuilders of our communities.

Crime is a curable condition; only 5% of those who commit crimes are truly dangerous career criminals. The scientific process of risk assessment has been extremely successful in screening to make the proper distinction. Bob Marley sang about the social problems existing in ghettoes and shantytowns across the globe. Nearly 40 years later, there is still so much trouble in the world, only now we have a clear understanding of what is needed to cure it. But can we find the will?

Vignette 3 "Welcome to Tunica Hills"

And now the sounds of grief begin to fill
My ear; I've come where cries of anguish smite
My shrinking sense, and lamentation shrill

A place made dumb of every glimmer of light,
Which bellows like tempestuous ocean birling
In the batter of a two-way winds buffet and hurling.

When they are borne to the rim of the ruinous path
With cry and wail and shriek they are caught by the gust, Railing and
cursing the power of the Lord's Wrath.

Dante Aligheri
The Divine Comedy: Hell
Translated by Dorothy L. Sayers
Penguin Books, Baltimore, Maryland 1949

SECTION 3

Welcome to Tunica Hills

The bus ride to Louisiana State Prison was uneventful. Because of my earlier escape attempt, I was transported at night with a full escort. The night travel lessened my ability to take in the sights, but not totally. I gave close attention to the cars we passed and tried to keep up with landmarks, until the driver turned off and started using back roads to reach our destination.

The roads we travelled took us deep into very dense darkness, earlier I had spotted signs that warned of wild bears and deer crossings. Now there were no more signs, passing cars, nor any hint of human life period. It began to feel like we were riding into a blackhole, an entryway to the gates of purgatory. After a while, we reached a crossroad and the driver turned left, the final stretch was about 22 miles down a road that ends at the front gate of Louisiana State Penitentiary, the French inspired penal colony better known as, Angola.

The plantation style prison sits approximately 200 miles northeast of New Orleans and rest snuggly against the muddy banks of the mighty Mississippi River. Surrounded by water on three sides, the former slave breeding farm was carved in the middle of the desolate Tunica Hills wilderness, at 18,000 acres it is about the size of Manhattan Island.

At the time of my arrival the institution was operating under the guidelines of a federal consent decree that arose from a lawsuit, (Williams v. McKeithen, 939 F.2d 1100), filed by inmates complaining of living conditions so deplorable and inhumane, Angola was dubbed, "the bloodiest prison in America". When the bus jerked to a stop the ferryman prison guard turns towards me and the other bus riders and announces, "well fellows you've made it to your final destination". With that he laughs and through his mirth sputters a few jokes about not dropping the soap. His glee at our circumstances made me remember, a passage from poetry by Dante' Aligheri, which reads:

> When they are borne to the rim of the ruinous path
> With cry and wail and shriek they are caught by the gust
> Railing and cursing the Power of the Lord's Wrath.

As we disembarked from the bus the reality of my situation hit me with increasing clarity. By the time we made it through the gates, the initial orientation and classification for housing, I knew exactly where we had come. Late that night when the cell door was closed behind me I laid on the bunk in the darkness, stared at the blank ceiling and whispered to myself, "I'm in Hell".

Clinical psychologists have posited that there are 10 stages of grief. These include the initial shock of the loss, and the emotional expression that follows. Depression and loneliness are, often accompanied by physical symptoms of distress, like weight loss. Some people begin to panic and have feelings that they are losing their minds. Panic is followed by guilt, then comes hostility, resentment, and anger.

During the days that followed, my dark depression was transformed to a white-hot anger, a burning rage, born of the grief I experienced in the traumatic loss of my God given liberty. I needed a way to express my anger, and since I wasn't at that time using writing as a form of self-therapy back then, I chose to take it out on the prison administration. I made up my mind to show my disdain for what I saw as an unjust system by challenging the security apparatus at every turn.

One day when the inmates on my unit were allowed outside on the very small cell block yard, I found myself searching for a way to engage a staff member in some type of altercation, verbal or physical it really didn't matter to me. There was a cadet on the yard with us, a white guy who lived with his family here at the prison all his life, the neighborhood inside the prison gate is called B-line. He was the kind who would openly use racial epithets like, "nigger" to get the Black guys moving when they were out of line. I moved close to the fence, so he would be forced to say something, and sure enough he fell for it.

"Hey Nigger, get your ass away from that fence"!
I shouted back, "Fuck you"!

He could not believe it. I could tell by the way his mouth was hanging open that he did not expect that reply. For a moment, he appeared to be stuck in the valley of decision. Prison guards in Louisiana do not carry guns inside the fences and I was honestly prepared to physically defend myself if he was inclined to take it there. Just as I thought he would, he reached down and activated his distress beeper, desperate for backup.

It took the response team almost 5 minutes to come to their comrade's aid. They arrived on the yard blown out, huffing and puffing as though they had just completed the Boston Marathon.

The leader was a fat middle aged white guy with a receding hairline and a ruddy complexion that exposed his swelling veins, clogged by the plaque that accompanies years of hog crackling consumption.

Nevertheless, his was the voice of unchallenged authority. "What in the hell is going on?" I thought to myself, *at least he knows where we are.* He looked at the cadet expecting an explanation for the code red distress signal. The cadet points at me and whines, "He cussed me."

The lead officer looks at me and takes in my, clean shaven face and innocent expression. He turns back to his officer and askes, "Why didn't you just write him up?"

With so many of his coworkers around he around he seemed ashamed and I almost began to feel sympathy for him, until he spoke again. His choice of words he used to explain shocked even me. He turns to his supervisor with the look of a son imploring his father to have some understanding and says, "Sir, this nigger told me to fuck myself."

Wow! He just gave me six witnesses to his use of a racial slur and total lack of professionalism. Although, lots of people in the United States like to pretend that they live in a post-racial society, the fact of the matter is racism is alive and well all across America, but the state of Louisiana operates a legal system not much different than South Africa during the era of aparthied.

My plan was to use this incident as a platform to air my grievance that the use of racial slurs by Angola staff members is grossly unprofessional and potentially jeopardizes the overall security of the institution. The trick was getting through this without any broken bones or being found dead hanging from the bars of my cell. Without looking in my direction the supervisor turns to one of his subordinates and orders him to lock me in a boot tier in Administrative Segregation. A boot tier is a cell with a solid door in front, once the outer door is closed an offender can be placed submerged in total darkness for as long as the tier officer decides.

They handcuffed me and lead me away to the boot. The cell they placed me in had no mattress or running water. When the guard closed the door, I was instantly enveloped in womb like darkness. I was engulfed in a cold black womblike silence, that caused me to experience a loss of equilibrium and a sensory malfunction that made me feel like I was spinning. I sat down on the cold hard slab of steel and thought to myself, *this is a fine mess you've gotten yourself into this time.*

Essay 1: Phantoms

"The Louisiana Justice System is primarily an organization for killing Black people."

Victor Damone McClendon

For my part, I would alarm and caution even the political and business readers that the essay, PHANTOM: THE BY-PRODUCT OF LOUISIANA'S "DEATH BY INCARCERATION" STRATAGEM, cuts to the heart of the matter and makes no apologies for its suigeneris nature. It was the writer's deliberate intent to convey the message that we, meaning those of us being unjustly held captive by a Slave State, can and will continue to make our presence felt and our plights known to the world.

There is s stygian form of government operating under the guise of a criminal justice system in Louisiana. Over the years, it has efficaciously diminished the Black populace in the state by using institutional racism as judiciary means to take away our ability to not only vote, and contribute to the welfare of our families, but to reproduce as well. Similar, to the Black Codes used during the Jim Crow era, the state has codified immoral and discriminatory jurisprudence to suit its overly ambiguous criminal code of procedures. My esteemed colleague, Curtis Ray Davis II, and I are socially dead. We are without a doubt "poltergeists" in a ghostly world of lost souls, trapped in a hell created by White Supremacist with the simple intention of making sure that Black men stay in a State of Slavery post the 1864 emancipation of the African slaves in the United States. We fervently believe that, when justice is not given, it must be demanded and taken, *by any means necessary.*

Victor Damone McClendon, Co-author of this Essay

"The United States will be made safer by remaining true to our values...we do not torture." Those were the words of President 'Barack Obama in explaining the nation's need to close the military prison camp at Guantanamo Bay, Cuba. With the country's dismal record on incarceration, U.S. Diplomats are having a hard time at the United Nations convincing other world leaders of the veracity of our claim of being a nation of high ideals and moral values.

Understandably, President Obama has his hands full as he and his staff must address pressing issues such as, the economy, the war on terror, and healthcare reform; however, it should be duly noted that the current prison crisis in "the land of the free" is and has been a giant elephant in the room. Over the years there have been literally thousands of articles written about the need for penal reform in the State of Louisiana and the effects of the state's historical practice of human warehousing. This essay; however, is intended to aid the reader in understanding the underlined nature of the problem and show more clearly how the Prison Industrial Complex (PIC) has transmogrified the moral conscience of the United States Government.

WHAT'S IN A NAME?

Who are we? We are no one. Our hopes and dreams have been deferred for reasons we may never fully understand. The intricate workings of Louisiana's Napoleonic criminal system of justice have facilitated our wrongful convictions as well as those of many others. This system is purposely disguised and hidden form the eyes of the world. Why?

According to H.R. Haldeman who was quoted in Lockdown America, former President Richard Nixon emphasized that, "…You have to face the fact that the whole problem is really the Blacks. The key is to devise a system (of justice) that recognizes this while not appearing to." Racial disparities (the number of Blacks to Whites) in America's prisons have reached epic proportions. The good news is the Obama administration brings to Government a new transparency policy that allows other nations to get a glimpse a Lady liberty without her make-up. Many are finding she is not so appealing after all. President Obama, understanding the ethnic insensitivities held by his predecessors, has commissioned a panel to investigate the race disparity in the nation's prisons and reported their findings to Congress. Everyone who profits from the P.I.C. will soon be under intense scrutiny… and now they know the world is watching.

Similar, to how greedy CEOs brought the banking industry to its knees, overzealous lobbyist and special interest groups used the umbrella of "public safety" to create and maintain a sort of capitalistic criminal justice system in the United States. This is a huge deal because it has amounted to a form of genocide or legal ethnic cleansing designed to stop or control reproduction of distinct racial or ethnic groups, which is an international war crime. Remember when Michael Vick went to jail for the mistreatment of animals; Louisiana is in the business of the warehousing human beings for profit and racial subjugation. This state has a very long history of torturing its poorest citizens, not for public safety, but to maintain the racial pecking order. How cruel is that?

Prolonged incarceration is sometimes referred to as "Social Death", so in a real sense, those of us sentenced to LWOP are, actual phantoms. In Louisiana, death by incarceration begins with the replacement of your name with a set of numbers, issued to you as you enter the purgatorial gates of the Louisiana State Penitentiary known as Angola. Once inside, your only mediums of private communication lie within hallowed, semi-secluded *seances* called attorney visits or the judiciary Ouija boards commonly known as "legal mail".

Although everyone comes to Angola, dead on arrival (DOA), you eventually discover that all phantoms are not the same. There are those who vehemently refuse to go quietly into the night. Their souls are restless because they are here by unjust means. These tormented spirits are relentlessly unwilling to allow their cries of injustice to be silenced by the system that caused their social demise. Instead, they make their presence known and their voices heard in the world they left behind. Opposed to phantoms, these bellicose spirits can be considered poltergeists or noisy ghost. The fact that you are reading this essay is proof that we really exist.

The deliberate taking of young, strong, black males for the purpose of working in plantation fields in the Southern United States is not a new concept in the America. If you are serious about understanding why there are so many Blacks in prison, then it would behoove you to look back at how it all began.

The Atlantic slave trade removed approximately 11.7 million people from West and Central Africa, with the sole intention of using them as slaves in Europe and the Americas. It was the successful cultivation of the tobacco in Virginia and Maryland that created the tremendous demand for labor and ultimately a lucrative industry was born, fueled by the blood, sweat and tears of Black people.

After the emancipation of the so-called Negro, American capitalist devised new plans on how they would keep their agricultural industry and way of life intact. A former confederate officer by the name of Samuel James was granted a contract with the State of Louisiana the allowed him a monopoly on convict labor for 20 years. He invented the convict leasing system and bought the 18,000 acres that became known as Angola. Some say the system he created was worse than slavery because with the ready supply of Negros to convict of crimes there was no longer any incentive to keep them healthy. He was also able to convince the Louisiana legislature to create a law that would allow a jury to convict a defendant even if 3 members of a 12-person panel believed that the case had reasonable doubt. A practice that has lasted for over a hundred years.

Essay 2: Humanitarian exercise or Slavery?

The period of history between the Louisiana Purchase, statehood and the Civil War was the time and space historians and antebellum scholars call "the Golden Age of Louisiana". For people who were not bound by the chains and shackles of slavery, it was an era of tremendous economic prosperity. The confederate aristocracy portrayed an image of wealth, refined culture and gentility. However, beneath this illusion lay the fact that the comfort and material extravagance was made possible by the exploitation, misery and hardships of hundreds of thousands of African slaves.

Then came the good ole' 13th Amendment: "Neither slavery nor involuntary servitude, except as a punishment for a crime where of the party shall have been duly convicted, shall exist within the United States or any place subject to their Jurisdiction."

Wait just one second. Does this mean that slavery was never really "abolished"? To the legal layman here is an announcement: Slavery is in perfect present tense time legal and in existence throughout the United States; whenever you are convicted of a crime. For the first time since the 1830s there are more than 2.3 million men, women and children living their lives in a condition of state sponsored slavery or involuntary servitude.

The Civil War was fought for economic reasons surrounding the taxation of Black slaves owned by Southern planters who had amassed vast fortunes as well as an international trade advantage over their Northern competitors. In 1857, Hinton Rowan Helper authored, "The Impending Crisis", which attacked the institution of slavery on moral and economic grounds. He believed that slavery was bad because it hurt the economic growth of poor white people who did not own slaves. His enemies declared him an agent of the North sent to sow disunity among the white people of the South. Ultimately, the book was banned, and copies were seized and burned.

Helper argued that slavery was a "disgrace to civilization" and pointed towards the sadistic, demonic behavior of the overseers and slave masters as evidence. The "peculiar" institution had been defended by the slave holders on a humanitarian exercise argument where the Massahs and Miss

Anns were cast as great paternal caretakers of illiterate, subhuman, dark-skinned beasts of burden they referred to as Niggers.

According to "Louisiana: A study of Diversity", in 1860, 50 percent of the people living in the state were slaves and 100 percent of those slaves were Black. It is also of interest to note that slave ownership in the state of Louisiana was not the exclusive privilege of the whites. In New Orleans alone approximately 750 free persons of color, known as gens de couleur libres, owned slaves. Brings-to-mind, the words of Public Enemy's front man Chuck D, "Every brother ain't a Brotha, cause of color".

It is now 2008 and we are all so enlightened and conscious that we know the arguments of the

19th century Southern Planters were simply wrong and immoral. Human beings should not be exploited for money based on race or anything else. The purposeful miseducation of the Black slave created an illusion of sub-human mentalities that the bad guys used to justify the slave sentence of social death.

Therefore, if the reader can agree in her heart and mind that slavery was morally and spiritually wrong, then why are you, with all this conscious talk not doing anything about it? Yesterday it was the so-called Negro; today it is anyone duly convicted of a crime. There are currently over 2.3 million slaves incarcerated throughout our Nation's modern-day plantations, work farms, prisons and correctional facilities.

Those laborers of the 18th and 19th centuries toiled in their agricultural and industrial purgatories, slaving form "can't see morning, to can't see night" for Massah's enterprise. Those human being were allotted no opportunity for self-improvement, education or social development.

The inmates of today toil in industrialized workshops, making everything from license plates to computer chips; these modern-day slaves pick crops in the South, tele-market wares in Arizona and die fighting wildfires in California. In the ole' days, most of the people accepted the arguments of the slave holders, who said that exploiting the uneducated social misfit that they housed, fed and clothed was a humanitarian exercise. A large amount of the inmates in the 21st century Prison Industrial

Complex are uneducated social misfits being housed and fed by benevolent governors and wardens.

Why does the change in labels and titles for those who warehouse human beings and exploit their labor now make the practice morally correct and acceptable? Why does the change in titles of those involved in this so-called humanitarian exercise make today's model and practice anything less than slavery?

Essay 3: Behind Enemy Lines

There is an age-old notion that good writing is born in tortured isolation which has become an almost universally accepted fact. One would need only look towards the past and identify the titans of the art of political wordsmithing to prove this point. After all everything is ultimately political. Writers dating back to the Mystery Schools of ancient Africa have demonstrated that the pen of the man of words is a greater weapon than the modern-day nuclear bomb.

Some of the greatest literary works in existences were created inside of cells. Whether monasteries, prisons, dungeons, or gulags, there is no doubting the fact that these voices, these words from the wilderness express the wisdom that is born of long suffering and impact us in ways that other work simply doesn't. For example, the majority of the New Testament of the Christian Bible was written by the apostle Paul from deep within the bowels of a prison cell.

Trosky and Lenin developed their interpretations of the writings of Karl Marx and Fredrick Engels inside the miserable gulags of Russia. The rhetoric of the infamous Adolf Hitler became a manifest reality only after her authored *Mein Kampf*; during his prison stay in Germany. The words and letters of Nelson Mandela sustained the spirits of the African National Congress and South African masses, from a tiny cage on Robben Island.

The list goes on and on; Mumia Abu Jamal, Stanley "Tookie" Williams, Wilbert Rideau and so many others, suffice it to say that once the political thinker is locked away physically, the perimeters of his mind and spirit expands. These austere conditions of incarceration have been known to either crush the will of the inmate/prisoner or bring forth a level of enlightened thought or self-realization that only a complete separation from the world can facilitate. I have experienced this epiphany, this call to write. A thirst to enter the dialogue and influence public opinion. I think I know a little something about suffering. At the time of this writing I have been incarcerated for 18 years for a crime that I didn't commit.

The story of prison is a story of letters, writs, grievances and appeals. I live in a place where one must write in, order to fight. I live in Louisiana State Penitentiary, better known as Angola. This is about as far behind enemy lines as a Blackman from Compton, California can dream of ever finding himself.

Angola was originally a slave breeding plantation it sits on 18,000 acres of the most fertile farmland in the United States. There are some who believe that the quality of the soil is so rich that you can cut off a human finger, plant it in the ground and grow a new person. Land wise, it is the largest maximum-security prison on earth and houses inmates who have been sentenced to the longest terms handed out by any known criminal justice system. Surprisingly, there has never been a major riot or prison uprising in the institution's history. We can most likely attribute this to the system of slave mental maintenance developed by Willie Lynch still being employed by the modern-day wardens and overseers.

Essay 4: Louisiana Back to Business as Usual?

On April 8, 1812, Louisiana became the 18th state to be admitted to the United States. Her traditions and heritage are grounded on a gumbo of the 18th century French and Spanish culture, seasoned with the spices of labor exploitation (slavery) and Aristocratic Racial hierarchy (Confederate Rebels). While most of society has moved past those times, Louisiana is the only state that is divided into Parishes instead of counties. Down here in the "boot" they put the images of racism/white supremacy up front and in your face. Sometimes it has nooses hanging from trees or trucks, more often you can see it in the 'fleur-de-lis' (the slave brand symbol on the Saints helmet) or the Rebel Flags all over the place.

I am an African American. I was 'captured' in Compton, California on September 18, 1990. I was flown by plane to Louisiana, tried for a shooting I can 'prove' I did not commit, wrongfully convicted and sentenced to Life in Prison. All in a courtroom that flew a Confederate battle flag alongside the Stars and Stripes. So, I consider myself an expert of sorts on the "injustice of Louisiana's Criminal Justice System". I imagine that my experience would evoke the same sense of Justice, Trust, and Fairness that a Jewish person might feel in a courtroom flying a flag emblazoned with a Swatztika

Last month the nation seemed shocked to find that Jim Crow had sired a son, (Jim Crow Jr.); down here we like to call him "Jimbo" or sometimes "Little Jimmy". The Civil Rights movement may have silenced Jim Sr., but Little Jimmy, with his bachelor's degrees and political clout can legislate discriminatory policy that constitutes 'legal lynching' on a scale that dear ole dad and his, cross burning buddies could only dream about.

Please do not be surprised to find prosecutors like Reed Walters of Jena, Louisiana boasting of destroying black lives, "with the stroke of a pen". They have used that power in the Louisiana Criminal Justice System since the days they made Vagrancy Laws to supply plantation labor to support their agricultural economy. The state numbers on Black/White sentencing practices is so lopsided; it has become the subject of political discussions across the country.

By giving protest to the Jena 6 case, Jesse Jackson, Michael Baisden, and Al Sharpton brought greater attention to the institutional racism in Louisiana's Criminal Justice System. Hopefully all those brothers and sisters from across the nation did not leave without realizing that there are literally hundreds of Michael Bells and Reed Walters down here.

A Life Sentence in Louisiana is known by the locals as "Death by Incarceration". It is sinister and diabolical but there exist, no viable release mechanism for a person sentenced to life for a violent crime. Louisiana has per capita the highest incarceration rate on the planet Earth. This statistic includes comparisons to South Africa, Russia, Saudi Arabia, China, Iran, and Egypt, with 836 per 100,000 capita of its citizens locked away and 82% of those black, the stats alone should warrant a United Nations Humanitarian Rights Counsel investigation to look at it as a rather ingenious form of ethnic cleansing.

I am live from ground zero keeping you aware and awake to the fact that Louisiana's confederate traditions are working to deprive many wrongfully convicted men and women of our Constitutional, Civil, and Human Rights. Some might say that arguing over procedure instead of releasing a man who is innocent sounds unfair, unjust, draconian, or just mean spirited. However, here in the 'boot' it is just business as usual, the good ole Louisiana way.

SECTION 4

Vignette # 4 Isolation

Within 72 hours of being placed in administrative segregation I was taken before a disciplinary board. After stating my rights and hearing the lame defense offered by the inmate legal counsel who represented me, I was found guilty of "Threat to security", a catch all charge almost impossible to acquit one's self of because the credibility is always weighted on the side of the correctional officer. The board sentenced me to the super maximum-security housing unit, formally known as the Camp J, Management Program.

The application and scope of solitary confinement in the United States varies from state to state; however, I can state from experience that it is a form of torture much worse and with far longer effects than any physical pain that a person might encounter. The majority of inmates at the Louisiana State Penitentiary are housed in open bay dorms, nonetheless, there are also many dungeon style cell blocks that are used as a deterrent to misconduct according to the administration, but are actually a simple means of implementing draconian punishment in the contemporary world.

Each Camp, (C, D, and J), along with the Main Prison Complex has its very own dungeon, known officially as "Administrative Segregation", they vary from extended lock down units and closed cell restriction to working cell block units. Because all but 78 cells have open bars, where inmates can verbally interact with one another, they are not considered isolation or solitary confinement cells.

Camp J is Angola's main disciplinary unit. It has four buildings with 32 tiers that house so-called violators that the administration believes might be in need, of a higher degree of management. Each tier has 13 one-man cells, and the length of confinement usually corresponds with the severity of the violation. Nevertheless, the minimum sentence to the Camp J management program is 6 months.

According to Angola's official policy, "Louisiana State Penitentiary does not practice total isolation or sensory deprivation confinement." This eyewitness avers that the previous statement is not true. There are six tiers at Camp J that have isolation cells with solid steel doors right in front of the regular bars the mechanism is known as a boot. These doors can be closed by any guard working the tier and the light switch is his/hers to manipulate according to whatever mood fate might have placed them.

The guards on my tier seemed to always be in a foul mood. They would close the boot in front of the cell for the smallest perceived insult. One of the strangest unofficial offenses during my time in Angola was referred to as "reckless eyeballing", it happens by looking a guard directly in the eye. An inmate accused of the fore-mentioned could find himself plunged into darkness for the next 72 hours.

After about 3 months in isolation the walls around my cell began to squeeze my soul, but the walls around my broken heart casted a pitch-black shadow across the void of where my spirit used to be. The darkness was having a devastating effect on my mind. Weird thoughts began to enter my head:

> *How did it come to this? Here I am sitting in the dark sentenced*
> *to serve out the balance*
> *of my natural life for something I didn't even do. Why me? Where*
> *is the justice in this?*
> *Where is God? Everyone has turned their backs on me.*

I squeezed my eyes shut, afraid that I might start crying and lose control completely. Some hazy memory came to me about the importance of maintaining emotional control. I cannot recall where I learned that. I was sitting on the edge of a mental cliff overlooking an abyss of utter hopelessness and despair. That is when the solution dawned on me. I could very easily bring this ordeal to an end and be free of this prison, the low-life guards and all the rest of my problems in an instant. My mind sat back somewhere in my sub-conscious, nodding its head like, "Yeah, what took you so long? Why should you give the State of Louisiana and your detractors the pleasure of watching you suffer in sub-human confinement, day after day, month after month and year after year until you decay from age or disease takes your life?"

Indeed, suicide really did seem a more honorable death than passively submitting to a life as a 21st Century slave. A life sentence in Louisiana is considered a quasi-death penalty by legal scholars because lifers have not viable release mechanism short of death.

A mind can be a convincing tool and the more I thought about it, the more reasonable the idea began to appear. Then something strange happened. I stopped thinking. Sitting there with my eyes closed I slowly began to realize that the thoughts my mind were displaying were not being consciously generated by me. I realized this when I became conscious of the fact that it was me who was listening to my mind. I quickly deduced that if I was capable of objectively listening to these thoughts which were obviously being created by something other than me, then there must be some distinction between me and my mind.

My studies of mindfulness had taught me that the mind is not the soul. The mind is a tool used by the human being to make sense of the world of material form. The mind is like an arm or leg of the human body. It is brain activity motivated from factors that vary based on one's emotional, physical and spiritual condition. The soul on the other hand is present in the heart of all human beings. I learned to commune with the Divine by concentrating on my breathing then gradually letting go of my need to analyze everything. The darkness helped because thought is weak where darkness is thick. At first, I was able to stop thinking for only a few seconds at a time, but I eventually learned to clear my mind for very long period and instantly notice when negative thought tried to sneak up on me.

Although I am the grandson of a Baptist Minister, I was not raised in a religious environment. Of course, like the good Christian girl she was brought up to be, my mother introduced me to the Bible when I was around 3 years old. I was taught, "The Lord's Prayer" and to say "Jesus wept" before chewing any of the food that was placed before me.

I can recall how dis-satisfied attending Church made me feel. On most Sunday mornings Mama made it compulsory that me and my siblings be present at Sunday School, where an elderly Black woman related the stories of Adam & Eve, the flood, and the Crucifixion of Christ. When we asked too many inconvenient questions, she would banish us to the isolation of the hallway leading to the basement. On one occasion she was telling us the story of the Creation as recorded in the Book of Genesis. Her explanation of God as Alpha and Omega was extremely confusing to me as I could not wrap my head around her description of God as the beginning and the ending. How does something so all-encompassing have an ending? Where did God originally come into existence? Who died and left Him in charge?

Essay 1: The Ricky Davis Affair: A Hurricane Katrina Story

On Aug. 29, 2005, the U.S. Gulf Coast was struck by a monstrous Category 5 hurricane. Meteorologists gave her the name Katrina, which means to cleanse.

The storm of the century washed away a shroud of secrecy covering the decay of poverty and corruption that rested beneath the normally festive environment that marked the city of New Orleans as the last truly "European" city on Earth.* The catastrophic destruction and lackluster government response had people crying out in moral outrage that this level of third world poverty could actually exist in North America – which is kind of strange seeing as how for years millions from all over the world made their pilgrimage to "Sin City" to drown their hedonistic urges in the festivals and parades that give praise to the Roman God Bacchus, the week prior to the Christian holiday known as Lent.

Two years after Katrina, 60,000 protestors descended on the small Louisiana town of Jena to confront a district attorney who bragged about his ability to take lives "with the stroke of a pen" when he charged six Black high school students with attempted second degree murder for a fist fight stemming from racially motivated hazing from white students at the campus.

Eight years later the Supreme Court has taken notice that the U.S. death penalty might need to be abolished because of the arbitrary manner in which prosecutors are deciding who gets to get the needle, demonstrated by the fact that 50 percent of all death penalty cases in the entire U.S. come from a single parish in Northern Louisiana. (Google Caddo Parish District Attorney Dale Cox.)

Several watchdog organizations have raised serious concerns about the racial disparity in the way Blacks and Whites are being charged for crimes exhibiting similar behavior. In most cases involving a homicide, the decision to charge white suspects with manslaughter and Blacks with second degree murder is a disturbing practice that has amounted to 89 percent of those serving life in Louisiana being people of color. Maybe the former has something to do with the fact that 98 percent of the state's 66 parishes have white men in the position of district attorney.

Hurricane Katrina made the situation much worse when most of the evacuees from New Orleans were Black people, pushed by the storm, into the more conservative Northern parishes, where law enforcement officials took a very hostile approach to dealing with what they saw as an invasion of "outsiders."

> The Supreme Court has taken notice that the U.S. death penalty might need to be abolished because of the arbitrary manner, in which prosecutors are deciding who gets to get the needle.

In a very interesting case in point, a New Orleans evacuee living in a Baton Rouge hotel was arrested and sentenced to life for fatally wounding a suspected serial rapist while trying to make a citizens' arrest. The "victim" was a local white man with political ties. His name was Corey Hawkins and the defendant a Black man with no criminal record named Ricky Davis.

Mr. Davis was one of the many thousands of people who did not leave New Orleans ahead of the storm. Once the levees broke, he suddenly found himself in a modern day, city of Ninevah, bodies floating in the streets and desolation everywhere. He worked his way through the makeshift refugee camps and two months after the storm was living in a roach motel in Baton Rouge.

On Oct. 29, 2005, exactly 60 days after the storm hit, Ricky Davis was sitting in his hotel room at the antebellum named Plantation Inn Hotel, when he was sought out by two female Katrina evacuees who had reported to the police that they had been raped by a white sexual predator. According to the ladies, the police "weren't doing anything" to protect them, and they were frightened even more because the suspect was seen lurking in the parking lot just a few minutes prior.

Ricky gave his cellphone to his girlfriend and instructed her to call the police and proceeded to the parking lot with the intention of detaining the suspect until the police arrived.

After arriving at the parking lot, witnesses pointed out the alleged predator stalking in a parked car. Mr. Davis confronted the suspect, informing him that several young Black females had accused him of rape.

The situation escalated when the alleged rapist attempted to shoot Mr. Davis and run over him with his car.

Hawkins subsequently died as a result of what was most likely a self-inflicted gunshot; however, in a remarkably amateurish investigation by local detectives, police failed to conduct a routine ballistics check on the weapon found in the victim's lap.

> Several watchdog organizations have raised serious concerns about the racial disparity in the way Blacks and Whites are being charged for crimes exhibiting similar behavior.

Ricky Davis was arrested and charged with manslaughter because of the mitigating factors of the case. That changed once the Hawkins family complained to their fellow Baton Rouge friends and contacts in the DA's office. The sentiment went something like this:

"How can an 'outsider' come to our parish and make a 'citizens' arrest? He's not a citizen of Baton Rouge; he's a damn refugee."

Before long the family successfully convinced the DA's office to upgrade the charge to second degree murder. The process by which the prosecutor used a "non-jury indictment" to make the upgrade is currently under review in the state's highest court. A crime that has a mandatory life sentence can only be implemented by a grand jury consisting of nine members.

The DA and the foreman in this case are alleged to have just signed the thing themselves without bothering to run it by the body. Ricky Davis went to trial and was found guilty as charged with a 10-2 jury verdict. Did I forget to mention that Louisiana is the only state where one can lose his freedom forever without having to have the U.S. gold standard of a unanimous verdict?

> Ricky Davis was arrested and charged with manslaughter because of the mitigating factors of the case. That changed once the Hawkins family complained to their fellow Baton Rouge friends and contacts in the DA's office.

The good ole' boy system runs deep and, whether right or wrong, a Blackman who takes the life of a white person is doomed to meet the wrath of Confederate-inspired Southern justice.

According to Michigan State Police Trooper Jeffery Werda, who gave an interview to the Associated Press: "I was told that I could go ahead and beat someone down or bitch slap them, and they would do the report. I was told this was my gift from them for helping with the hurricane relief efforts.

"Comments were also made throughout the night by the Baton Rouge officers that they were told by their commanding officer to harass the evacuees from New Orleans because they wanted them to leave Baton Rouge."

Because of such attitudes from local law enforcement it is clear, that Ricky never had a chance of receiving fairness in such a toxic judicial environment. The Ricky Davis affair is just one of the little known, travesties that has arisen as a result of the storm.

In Louisiana, a life sentence means you die in prison. Mr. Davis' act of heroism has turned him into a victim of an arbitrary racially motivated legal lynching. If Black Lives Matter, it's hard to tell down here in Louisiana.

> In Louisiana, a life sentence means you die in prison. Mr. Davis' act of heroism has turned him into a victim of an arbitrary racially motivated legal lynching.

*New Orleans reminds many of an old school world that no longer exists anywhere on earth, not even in Europe. Although New Orleans is in the U.S., it is different from any other place for the things that can be done there and the way the people act.

Essay 2: Louisiana Must Decarcerate

In 2007, this reporter wrote an article entitled, "Louisiana: Back to business as usual?" wherein I described the Jena 6 movement in the following terms:

A crowd of 600 turned out for the Decarcerate Louisiana rally on April 20, far more than the 250 the organizers expected. Youth were well represented.

"Last month the nation seemed shocked to find out that Jim Crow has sired a son, Jim Crow Jr.; down here, we like to call him "Jimbo" or sometimes "lil Jimmy." The Civil Rights Movement may have silenced Jim Sr., but Lil Jimmy, with his bachelor's degree and political clout, can legislate discriminatory policy that constitutes "legal lynching" on a scale that dear ol' dad and his cross burning, buddies could only dream about."

Not much has changed since 2007. Louisiana remains the lead incarcerator on the planet Earth and, even in post-Obama America, the legal system is being used as a weapon against Black people with arbitrary strokes of pens that take away lives as sure as a genocide or legal holocaust.

What has changed is the attitude of the people of Louisiana, who, on April 20, 2017, took over the steps of the Baton Rouge capitol and demanded that their lawmakers reallocate resources that have traditionally been squandered in the criminal justice system and put them back into education and hospitals.

Not much has changed since 2007. Louisiana remains the lead incarcerator on the planet Earth and the legal system is being used as a weapon against Black people with arbitrary strokes of pens that take away lives as sure as a genocide or legal holocaust.

Louisianans for Prison Alternatives is a coalition of over 16 organizations working together to make sure that this regular session of the Louisiana Legislature marks the beginning of the end for Louisiana's dubious distinction as the world's highest incarcerator. John Burkhart, director of the Southern Poverty Law Center, says that his organization will remain in Baton Rouge until the session ends on June 8 to make sure that the legislators do what they are recommended to do by the Governor's Task Force slated with the job of figuring a way out of this quagmire.

What has changed is the attitude of the people of Louisiana, who, on April 20, 2017, took over the steps of the Baton Rouge capitol and demanded that their lawmakers reallocate resources that have traditionally been squandered in the criminal justice system and put them back into education and hospitals.

Never in the history of Louisiana has the public made such an outcry, in regards, to penal reform. Organizational leaders fanned out through the capitol talking to surprised senators and state reps who seem very unfamiliar with the voice of the ordinary people whom they are supposed to be representing. When confronted by one activist, who asked a senator, "Why do you support death by incarceration?" he responded that he had never heard of such a thing.

A life sentence in Louisiana is known by the locals as "death by incarceration." It is sinister and diabolical because even though it is only a quasi-death penalty, under law there is no viable release mechanism for a person sentenced this way for any crime of violence.

When confronted by one activist, who asked a senator, "Why do you support death by incarceration?" he responded that he had never heard of such a thing.

Louisiana has per capita the highest incarceration rate in the world. This statistic includes comparisons to South Africa, Russia, China, Saudi Arabia, Iran and Egypt. And with 87 percent of these people being Black, the United Nations Human Rights Council should be investigating Louisiana's legal system as a rather ingenious form of ethnic cleansing. Louisiana must decarcerate – or accept the fact that this is modern legal apartheid.

Essay 3: An Ex-Convict Challenges Caddo Sheriff Prator's Tough Talk

During Caddo Parish Sheriff Steve Prator's recent press conference, he raised the same fears that filled Louisiana's prisons and broke Louisiana's budget and Louisiana's communities apart.

The state spends nearly $700 million annually on corrections, but one in three inmates released from prison returns within three years. Our sheriff said he is "as compassionate as anyone," but that he is not in the "rehabilitation business."

So why is he holding a press conference to scare our community instead of working with inmates in his custody in a way that aids in effective change?

I was released from Angola Prison on July 8, 2016, after serving nearly 26 years for second-degree murder, for which I was wrongfully convicted — that is, approximately one year and three months ago — and during the entire time I have been gainfully employed as well as a student at Southern University.

I was released from Angola Prison on July 8, 2016, after serving nearly 26 years for second-degree murder, for which I was wrongfully convicted — that is, approximately one year and three months ago — and during the entire time I have been gainfully employed as well as a student at Southern University.

I have worked tirelessly throughout Shreveport to change the mentality of our young people that crime is cool, and I will continue to provide the gift of my experience to people who might otherwise be forced to walk through a criminal justice system more interested in punishment and profiteering than solving the problems that create crime in the first place.

I am an example of one of "these people" who spent time in prison and am now making it despite all the obstacles people like Sheriff Prator put in front of us.

The Louisiana Justice Reinvestment Task Force is a bipartisan group comprised of law enforcement, court practitioners, community members and legislators, that found that Louisiana's corrections system is producing low public safety returns at very high cost.

Maybe if Sheriff Prator spent less time in front of the cameras and more time working with inmates to prepare them to be good neighbors and citizens, we wouldn't have to be fearful of the reforms our state so badly needs.

EPILOGUE

"A butterfly is God's proof that you can have a second chance at life."

—*Author Unknown*

After a ridiculously difficult amount of legal maneuvering in 2014, I was able to convince the Louisiana Supreme Court that my conviction and sentence were indeed a travesty of justice. Nevertheless, that did not mean that the State would just apologize and let me go. I was remanded to Caddo Parish District Court for an evidentiary hearing to test the veracity of my claims against the State.

It was surreal to find myself outside of the gates of Angola for the first time in a quarter of a century. The ride in the back of the transport vehicle allowed me to see a completely different world than the one that I had left so long ago. Watching the people in their cars speaking to thin air (Bluetooth), while waiting on the lights to change was miraculous to me. Just taking it all in was a herculean task in and of itself. Louisiana had grown. Once completely rural areas were now bustling townships and small cities. The poorest state in the U.S. had seemed to come a very long way.

By the time we finally made it to court I was completely exhausted, certainly the wrong posture to have, when one is literally fighting for his life. The district attorney working to keep me unlawfully incarcerated was a gentleman by the name of Dale Cox, who later gained infamy for stating out loud that the state should work to kill more people. He met me in an ex parte' contact in front of my holding cell before the hearing began. "You are going to die in prison, and I am going to make sure of that." For the life of me I could not understand what was fueling his hate for me, after all we had never met before and he really didn't know that much about me. Instead of making a snide remark I simply replied, "We'll see."

It was time for me to cry for help. I immediately filed a motion for continuance because the court appointed lawyer that was assigned to my case admitted that he had never conducted an evidentiary hearing for a post-conviction proceeding and therefore was of the opinion the we had no chance of winning the case. The judge agreed to give me 60 days to raise the money for competent counsel and I knew just who I needed. A few years earlier I'd read a writ of habeas corpus filed by a female attorney in New Orleans for a death penalty case. The sharpness of her mind and imagination was amazing to me. I promised myself that if I were to ever get back into court, I would do everything in my power to convince her to take my case.

Somethings are easier said than done...

As soon as I made it back to Angola, I contacted her. In my estimation, Rachel Conner is one of the best collateral review attorneys in the entire country. Therefore, I knew that getting her to take my case was not going to be easy, nevertheless, I learned a long time ago that a close mouth never gets fed. When I called and explained my situation her first response was basically there would be no way that she could handle it because her caseload was much too heavy. I explained to her that I was not your regular client. I didn't need her to do much legal work, what I needed more than anything was a person that could keep the Caddo Parish District Attorney's office from cheating me. All I was asking for was fairness.

Mrs. Conner eventually agreed to read the posture of my case and talk to me within a week. To my surprise she contacted me again within a few days and let me know that if I could afford her retainer that she would take the case. Of course, I couldn't afford to purchase a bar of soap at the time; however, I assured her that I would get the money. I had approximately 50 days to come up with what amounted to a down payment on a house.

Offenders sentenced to serve a "hard labor" incarceration in the state of Louisiana can earn incentive pay for working at prison jobs. The pay is 4 cents per hour, and 2 of those cents are kept by the state. So, an offender can work forty hours a week, every week for twenty years straight and make $8,320 and that if he or she is able to save every penny. Therefore, working one's way out is not a viable option. Then there is the black market: drugs, cigarettes, extortions, gambling, etc. However, there is a slight problem with the Darkside, which is the real possibility of never making it home alive. But, how else can a person find the resources necessary to fight a winning case against the awesome power of the State? I turned to friends and family for donations. After making over a hundred desperate calls all over the world I finally came up with the five-digit figure I needed for my attorney's retainer fee. Now I was ready for war. Mrs. Conner officially enrolled on my case as attorney of record.

It was then that she started to realize that, although I had an airtight application for post-conviction relief, there were politics surrounding my case that cause her to call in re-enforcements. That is when she brought, LSU Law School Professor James E. Boren to visit me at Angola. Professor Boren has written several textbooks on Post-Conviction Relief and collateral review proceedings, he is probably one of the top five appellate attorneys in the country. I consider him the Michael Jordan of appellate law.

The visit was a *tour de force*, on the science of post-conviction. We sat together in a small room for hours, going over strategies and options for my upcoming hearing. I decided that I wanted to consider another option. I believed that the DA's office would realize that they could not really win the case against me and would ultimately be out of a large amount of money if I was exonerated. My plan was to come into a mutual agreement or what is known as a joint motion with the state to allow me to plea guilty to a charge that would require my immediate release and not seek to prosecute my brother since I'd already served the time for the crime.

In the interim, Dale Cox was forced to step down as acting District Attorney of Caddo Parish and for the first time in its history, the people elected an African American to the most powerful law enforcement officer in the Parish. Judge James Stewart became District Attorney and launched a quiet investigation into the veracity of my conviction lead by Rod Demery, who found that it was more likely that not that the previous administration had convicted and sentenced an actually innocent man to serve out the balance of his life in Prison. On July 6, 2016 my team of attorneys and the Caddo Parish District Attorneys Office entered a Joint Motion that allowed me to enter a plea of Principal to Manslaughter, which call for my immediate release.

All and all I served 25 years and 9 months of my Life Sentence. Incidents of wrongful convictions happen so often nowadays that society seems to have become desensitized to the fact that men and women across the country are suffering the very real trauma of being wrongly incarcerated. For over a quarter of a century I remained very vocal about the fact that I did not commit the crime for which I had been convicted and sentenced to serve out the balance of my life, but it seemed that no one was interested. After all, everybody says that they didn't do it, right? I entitled this book, "Slave State" because that is the best way, I could describe both the place and the condition of my unlawful confinement.

As you hold this literary journey in your hands today, according to the 13th Amendment of the Constitution of the United States, slavery was never abolished. The institution that still allows the government to legally exploit the labor of anyone *"duly convicted of a crime"*, is just a means of keeping Black and marginalized people in our traditional place. Louisiana is a place that relishes the heritage of African Slavery. With almost 50% of it's population either in jail, prison, on probation, parole or an ex-convict, Louisiana is without any comparison, this is the true Slave State.